SWIFTLY THEY STRUCK

SWIFTLY THEY STRUCK

STRUCK

The Story of No. 4 Commando

BY

MURDOCH C. McDOUGALL

WITH A FOREWORD BY
BRIGADIER THE LORD LOVAT,
D.S.O., M.C.

ARMS AND ARMOUR PRESS
LONDON NEW YORK SYDNEY

The publishers wish to thank the following
for permission to reproduce photographs: The Imperial
War Museum, The Commando Association and Topical Press. Other
photographs are from the author's own collection.

Published in 1986 by Arms and Armour Press Limited,
2-6 Hampstead High Street, London NW3 1QQ.

Distributed in the USA by Sterling Publishing Co. Inc.,
2 Park Avenue, New York, N.Y. 10016.

Distributed in Australia by
Capricorn Link (Australia) Pty. Ltd., P.O. Box 665,
Lane Cove, New South Wales 2066, Australia.

First published in 1954 by Odhams Press Limited,
Long Acre, London.

British Library Cataloguing in Publication Data:
McDougall, Murdoch C.
Swiftly they struck: the story of No. 4 Commando. –
(Special forces library; V.4)
1. Great Britain, *Army. Commando*, No. 4 – History
2. World War, 1939–1945 – Personal narratives, British
I. Title   II. Series
940.54′81′41   D760.C6/

ISBN 0-85368-739-0

Printed and bound in Great Britain
by Billing and Sons Limited, Guildford, London
and Worcester.

Not heav'n itself upon the past has pow'r
But what has been, has been, and I have had my hour.
DRYDEN: *Paraphrase of Horace*

FOREWORD

WHEN I was first asked to write a foreword to a book about my old Commando it seemed an excellent idea and the promise was gladly given, for the author had chosen his time well and cunningly, long after midnight at a festive occasion in the Lowlands of Holland; the scene—a party in the Burgomeister's Office at Bergen-op-Zoom; a jeep-load of champagne was on the table, a fighting patrol had gone out for the oysters—the Rhine lay ahead and tomorrow was another day.

The picture has changed. Time has gone by and the gallant Commando has gone with it—broken up, cannibalized and finally disbanded as no longer necessary. Their name is not in the Army List, but you will find the headstones of the men that died to immortalize a name on every beach and battlefield in western Europe—the Flowers o' the Forest are a' wede awa'—the Green Berets have been handed back to store.

For over three years they had lived like twentieth-century pirates in a world of their own: ashore and afloat in harbours up and down the coast from St. Ives to the Outer Hebrides. For them the war had been a gay adventure: raiding the enemy coast a tonic: and exhaustive training (which required a constant change of scene) the sedative without which it was impossible to maintain morale and curb high spirits. The author of this book has traced some of our growing pains, difficulties and disappointments. Let no one imagine it is an easy task to raise and train five hundred men from different regiments, all strangers to each other, many of them misfits, mostly individualists, and get immediate results; in point of fact, more than a year elapsed before the Commando found its feet and began to pull together. First the turnout started to improve, then the men got fit—their fine physique made them invincible in representative games and they liked it; leaders were found—the duds were

7

eliminated; new weapons and equipment began to trickle in, landing-craft were provided to get on with the job.

Sailors talk about happy ships as well as lucky ones; we were certainly blessed with more than a fair share of these two priceless gifts: *esprit de corps* always characterized the unit; self-confidence came after winning our spurs at Lofoten, and that was the most important thing of all. The blade had been forged—it was to be kept keen by a series of large- and small-scale attacks on Hitler's Atlantic Wall. So a band of volunteers trained themselves first into a fighting formation, then into shock troops, finally to be given pride of place in Montgomery's order of battle as the spearhead of the B.E.F., the first troops ashore on D-day.

Numerically the Commando was not as big as a battalion, and at full strength consisted of twenty-five officers (including the M.O.) and 435 other ranks; but they all came under "starter's orders": every man went into battle fighting his particular weapon. Thus the Orderly-Room Corporal in my day was given a flame-thrower and fought with the best, while the office clerk carried a Bangalore torpedo as well as a typewriter to make the rough way smooth. We were a small but select party; casualties were inevitably severe; alas the best men were first to be killed, for they went in front. You will read how on the eighty-third day of the battle in Normandy the Commando, which had never been out of the line from 6 June, had lost over a hundred per cent of its original effective strength.

During the course of the war two V.C.s were won by men who passed through the ranks of No. 4 Commando. Their names are Captain Porteous, V.C., and Lieutenant Gardiner, V.C., M.C. The unit collected five D.S.O.s and eight of its officers rose to the rank of lieutenant-colonel and above. Curiously enough, not one of these was a Regular—a reminder to professional soldiers (and to politicians who discourage enterprise) not to take themselves too seriously. Subalterns and other ranks did as well and better in the long list of gallantry awards.

I have mentioned these facts in order to draw the wider

8

picture, for the author has modestly confined himself to the story of his own troop. If I have praised my comrades too highly I make no apology, for the men of No. 4 Commando were beyond all praise.

I welcome this book because it tells in simple language a good story that otherwise might be forgotten, for the world has a short memory; there are no heroics; Murdoch McDougall has looked on sudden death too often to make a fuss about it. His book leaves one with the feeling of a job well done and the echo of Napoleon's dictum—that bravery is never out of fashion.

LOVAT

CHAPTER I

*It was when the moon was setting
And the dark was over all.*

TENNYSON

SILENTLY the line of stocking-capped men moved along the narrow deck by the torpedo-tubes towards the davits, where hung the dory. They looked lumpy and grotesque in their reversible kapok jackets, which they would wear until they reached the shore, and instead of a face there seemed to be in each case simply a gap, for faces, ears and necks had been carefully smeared with sooty camouflage paint.

With a faint whirring the dory was lowered away and slapped softly into the water. A quiet word of command, and the little engine purred into life. Gradually the tiny craft thrust away from the parent ship, to be joined by a second one from the other M.T.B., then the two of them chuffed towards the light line which denoted the surf rolling on to the shore. The sound of their engines soon merged with that of the waves and the low outline of the dories disappeared from view, until they showed up again for a second as they entered the surf-line just prior to beaching.

I leaned back against the long torpedo-tube, while the signaller crouched by his set. We prepared for a wait of some four hours. It was Boxing-night of 1943 and bitterly cold. I glanced at my watch. Just after midnight. Back in the lonely house near Folkestone in which we had been living in impatience for several weeks Len Coulson and Peter Mercer-Wilson would have finished the nightly instalment of our marathon game of poker-dice, and would probably be listening to Peter's unvarying selection of Bing Crosby records, played over and over on his portable gramophone. Len was the commander of "F" troop, in which Peter and I were subalterns.

There was a faint crackling from the set on the deck. I could hear the voice from the shore: "Hallo Pat One. Message. Over."

Quietly the signaller answered: "Hallo Pat One. Pass your message. Over."

Again the crackling. "Hallo, Pat One. All okay so far. Starting phase two now. Will call only if things go wrong. Out." Starting phase two. That meant they'd landed and the two dories had got back out through the surf all right. The shore party would now be making their way up to and through the wire, once they'd tested it for mines.

The signaller reported the message to the nearest naval officer, who in turn reported it to the bridge. The sound of the water slapping against the sides of the ship seemed loud enough to be heard on shore, while the cold grew more intense each minute. I could see no sign of the two dories, which should by now be lying off somewhere fairly close, waiting for the call which would send them scurrying in again to pick up the shore party. Then there would follow the tricky business of bringing the full dories through the surf, which could be the very devil when troops were trying to embark.

I thought of Haw-Haw on the radio yesterday, reporting smugly: "Jairmany calling. A party of so-called Commando troops were caught attempting a landing on the coast of Holland yesterday. The group was liquidated." I wondered about that. It had been a party of French chaps, from the two troops of French who had recently been attached to us.

It had been the surf in their case, too, according to the M.T.B. people. The party had landed and after being on shore over three hours had signalled that they were about to return. Then apparently they had run into trouble. As the dory went shorewards to collect them, shots had been heard. From the M.T.B. very little could be seen, but soon in the line of surf they could make out the shape of the dory, with what appeared to be figures struggling round it. That had been all.

It was Christmas Day when we heard Haw-Haw. I

remembered the effect it had had on the Frenchmen with us. Most of them, having already suffered considerably at German hands, let loose a torrent of abuse at all things German, some shedding tears of emotion as they did so. One, however, said very little. I didn't know his name, as they had not been with us long, but he had a thoughtful, almost brooding, look, and his voice when he did speak was quiet and intense. He spoke English better than the others too, and while he lacked the boisterous bonhomie of his companions, there was a deep humour lurking behind the thoughtful eyes.

I gazed towards the shore. It seemed hellish quiet. I wondered what the sentries on the coast must be thinking as they wandered along their accustomed beat. Probably wishing the relief would hurry, or enjoying a furtive fag down behind some dyke. But a chap like that could be more trouble than the sort who walked regularly up and down his beat. There was more chance of his remaining unseen and he'd only to get one shot in to raise the alarm. Queer how things happened, one minute everything was as quiet as the grave, and the next——

"Christ!" said the naval officer. "What's that?"

The blackness of the shore was suddenly rent by a lurid orange flame and the silence shattered by the subsequent explosion.

"There'll be 'ell on nah," muttered one of the crew. "We'll 'ave 'alf the ruddy German Navy arter us."

An oppressive silence settled on the shore, and the darkness weighed like lead as we strained our eyes for any sign of movement. But the expected rattle of fire and the thump of grenades did not materialize. Nor was there any call for assistance from the shore party. I imagined them lying doggo, clinging to the sand of the dunes, waiting to see if the noise of the explosion would bring out a patrol.

"Wot d'yer s'pose it was?" hissed the matelot to the signaller.

"A mine, I should think, because the flash went up in the air an' not flat like a gun would go."

15

Minutes dragged by. Away over to the left a flare shot skywards and there came the sound of distant gunfire.

"Wonder wot *they're* playin' at," said the sailor.

"Probably the coastal guns practising," said the signaller. "They nearly caught us the other night by mistake."

I thought of the shock it had given us when a dark shape had passed across our bows some little way ahead, and shells had suddenly screamed towards us from the coastal guns, which apparently had chosen that night to indulge in target practice. We had lain-to for almost two hours before abandoning the thing and making our way home.

"Let's 'ope they don' switch rahnd 'ere," said the sailor fervently.

Again we settled down to wait, and time slipped freezingly by. There were still two hours to go, with an extra hour if the shore party didn't turn up at the appointed time. I strained my eyes towards the dark line of the coast, trying vainly to pierce the screen of darkness.

A searchlight suddenly stabbed out an accusing finger across the water on the starboard bow and began to flicker from side to side. The other M.T.B., which lay to our starboard beam, stood out silhouetted against the whiteness of the light. Then it swept on to us. I felt about fifteen feet high. The light was on a headland about a mile or so along the coast. There was known to be another one on the headland on the port side, and although it was unlikely that we could be seen from the shore in the beam of one light the two together might show us up to anyone using night glasses.

Should that happen and we still had to wait for the shore party we might quite well be cut off by E-boats, in which case we would have to make a running fight of it the whole way home.

The light continued to flicker and flash on the water for about another quarter of an hour, then it went out as suddenly as it had appeared. The tension on board our little craft relaxed. Another half-hour dragged by. There was less than an hour to go now. I was no longer cold. I was numb.

One of the sailors came padding round the narrow deck,

14

squatted down beside the signaller and stayed for a few minutes sharing our vigil. I wondered about Pat Porteous and his party ashore. They should soon be preparing for the return. I wondered if they would have a prisoner. That was why I was there at all. Pat's task tonight was a reconnaissance for a bigger landing the next night. That was our troop task, and because of the shortness of time between the reconnaissance and the raid I had been sent along with Pat's group to interrogate any prisoner he might take, so that I could report the results direct to Len Coulson on our return.

We had already made several abortive attempts to carry out a landing. The weather had been against us, with gales on one side or other of the Channel. Then there had been that business with the coastal guns and their target practice. Another night it had been the two searchlights, while on a third occasion the phosphorus on the water had so lit up the two M.T.B.s that they were as though floodlit, so we had had to turn back. This patrol of Pat's was to decide the whole thing. There was only one more night in the dark period of this month, so we had to go the next night or not at all, depending on the report brought back by the party at present on shore.

The friendly sailor stood up to continue his round. Suddenly he stopped, pointed out into the gloom and hissed: "'Ey, wot the 'ell's that?"

We both peered out in the direction indicated. Was it imagination, or was there really something dark on the water? I looked away, then brought my gaze slowly round in the direction of the supposed object, so that it would come into view in the corner of my eye first. Sure enough, there it was, a low black line on the surface of the water.

"There's something there," I admitted. The sailor waited for no more.

"It's a bloody U-boat," he said, and whipped off to report to the bridge. In the midst of the ensuing argument about the thing on the water the signaller's second set began to crackle. The message was from the two dories, who reported the presence of an E-boat between them and the M.T.B.s.

"Have you seen it for long?" asked the signaller.

"No, only a few minutes," came the reply.

Light dawned on the signaller.

"That's us, you idiot," he said, and reported to the bridge that the black object was probably the dories, which had put out some distance upwind and uptide, but had drifted down without knowing it, until they had suddenly seen the shape of what they took to be an E-boat looming up before them.

Further recriminations were cut short by the first set coming to life.

"Hallo Pat One. Coming back with one casualty. Send in for us now. Over."

"Hallo Pat One. Wilco. Out."

He passed the message on, then sent the dories in shorewards. Another period of waiting, then——

"Here they come."

The dories drew nearer and nearer, till they finally slapped and bumped alongside. The naval officer leaned over the side.

"How did it go?"

Back came the cheerful voice of Pat Porteous as the dory was swung inboard.

"Oh, all right. Someone trod on an S-mine and the damn thing didn't go off till we'd all passed, then it hit Corporal Richards in the back. He's O.K. though, and we got some sand, and a mine, and a bit of the wire."

"Right. Then we'll start for home."

I went down with Pat into the tiny wardroom. He stowed away his trophies, then looked up.

"Well, Mac, not much for you, I'm afraid. We never saw a soul."

He looked at the little collection he had just put down, shrugged his shoulders and said: "It makes you wonder if all this is really worth while, doesn't it? I suppose some clever sod'll work out some vital information from this lot."

Two minutes later he was sound asleep as the M.T.B.

thrashed and shuddered its uncomfortable way back to Dover.

We got there just after first light, and while Pat went off to make his report the rest of us piled into the waiting transport and went back to our lonely mansion in the country, where I reported to Len over breakfast. There was very little to say, and when I had finished Len said: "Well, I'll order a troop parade for two o'clock. They'll probably send us the word by the D.R. then, and I'll be able to tell them one way or the other at the parade. You'd better go and get some sleep, Mac, we'll give you a shout about dinner-time."

I nodded and rose from the table. I felt weary and a little depressed. "Any word of these French chaps?" I asked.

Len shook his head. "Not a thing," he said. "The M.T.B. went back last night and hung around waiting for a signal, but . . ." he shrugged. "It looks as though they've had it."

I went off to bed. It was two years before we discovered what actually had happened to those Frenchmen. They had been captured after the surf had overturned their craft, taken up the beach, made to dig a long trench, then they were shot and tossed into the trench they had dug, all in accordance with Hitler's order of October, 1942, which stated that all Commando troops taken, whether "in battle or not, in uniform or not, were to be shot out of hand." Papen, Schacht and many of the others who signed this order have since been whitewashed and released after serving a nominal sentence.

That afternoon the troop was drawn up on parade, and as Len appeared with a message form in his hand they were called to attention. Peter and I saluted. He returned the salute, stood us all at ease and said simply: "It's off. We're to go on leave." A short while later the disgruntled troop was dismissed, and we went to our room to pack our kit. From the direction of the troop's quarters came the sound of voices raised in raucous query: "Why are we waiting? Always —— well waiting!" Len jerked his head in the direction of the din.

"I'm not surprised they're browned-off," he said. "We've

17

been messing about on this business for two whole months now, and every time we get keyed up and all set to go some damn thing turns up."

"If they get enough beer on their leave they might be all right," I said. "What are you doing about yours?"

"I'll wire Jill to get leave and meet her in London," said Len. "Then we could have a drink together before we get the train home. What about you, Peter?"

Peter looked at the chaotic pile of kit all around him.

"I'll have to get this lot home I suppose. How is it I always seem to have so much more than you chaps?"

Len laughed. "You'd better leave these records at home this time," he said. "They're about worn out anyway."

"Rubbish," said Peter. "Where I go, they go, but we might get a couple of new ones. And, Mac, you can get some more poker-dice, the paint's worn right off these; that's how Len keeps winning."

Next morning we set off for London. The troop, still out-of-sorts at the cancellation of the operation, gradually came round as they neared the city. Most of them would forgather in some pub near the station, where they would drink together before separating to head for their various destinations.

At the entrance to Victoria Station we dumped our kit on the pavement and paused.

"What about Jill?" Peter asked. Len looked at his watch.

"She gets to Euston at about six this evening. What do you chaps want to do now?"

"The best thing is for you and me to get our kit across to King's Cross right away. Peter'll want to get his lot home, then we can have a meal or something and then all go and meet Jill."

"Fair enough," said Peter. We arranged where to meet and set out, Peter in the one direction, Len and I towards King's Cross.

Wallowing in a bath in one of the officers' clubs that afternoon I viewed the prospects of the leave. I was going to Edinburgh, where my mother and sister lived, my father having died before the war. I didn't suppose I'd see many of my friends, who were mostly either overseas or bombing half of Europe, but I hoped some of them might be on leave at the same time. I thought of Len. He was going to Newcastle with Jill, his wife, who was in the Wrens. Peter and I thought a lot of Jill, attractive, intelligent and unspoiled. She and Len were both lucky. Still I was damn glad I wasn't married, not in a war. There was enough to think about without any worries of that sort.

Len thundered on the door. "Come on, Mac, we've still to get a meal somewhere."

I splashed out. "All right. How about going to a Chinese restaurant?"

"Chinese . . . ? You heathens are all the same, what's the matter with this place?"

"Well, you get more in a Chinese restaurant."

"Never mind that, man. We'd better get to that place where we've to meet Peter. What was it called again?"

"It's a place off the Haymarket. I know where it is."

"What made you pick on it?"

"You get good pickled herrings there."

"What's the attraction about pickled herrings?"

I opened the door and we made for the stairs.

"They give you a thirst."

We met Jill at her station at six. Len looked slightly sheepish as she came along the platform. Peter and I waved. She waved back, handed us each a travelling bag, kissed Len, then looked round.

"Well, men?" she inquired. "Been looking after him all right?"

I looked down at her. "He's been working us to death," I said.

Peter frowned at her. "He's been winning all our pay at poker-dice," he said.

"Oh, goody!" said Jill. "Let's all go and celebrate."

That was the start of the leave. Next morning I was in Edinburgh.

For the first two or three days I went from one haunt to the next, trying to find someone I knew. None of the old crowd seemed to be at home this time; the town was full of strangers and allied troops, some of whom had become so at home in my favourite pub that they seemed to resent my occupying my former seat. I became slightly morose and began to look forward to going back to the unit.

I settled myself firmly against the bar, ordered a pint of beer and began to ruminate on Army life as it had affected me as an individual. At the outbreak of war I had just graduated from the university, where I had been studying languages. I had specialized in German, and so great had been my optimism in 1939 that I had taken a post with a firm in Leipzig, where I had been due to start on 15 September of that year. Knowing nothing of the Army, I had imagined that languages would be of some use, and had in answer to an advertisement in the paper travelled down to Mytchett, where, on the first of November, I was interviewed and accepted for something called Field Security. It was all very mysterious, and I was sent off home after the interview with the assurance that I would be sent for "within a fortnight." Six months later, after repeated letters to and fro, I finally reported to a ghastly barracks in Sheerness, where the cook was jailed for selling the rations and there were three lavatories for about two hundred and fifty men.

After some six weeks in this haven I was posted to a section and sent to embark for France. Halfway to the port of embarkation we were recalled and spent the next week or so helping to delouse innumerable Belgians and Frenchmen. Finally I was posted to a section which had returned from Dunkirk, and whose officer had been home a clear three days before his section. Fortunately he was soon promoted, and after a spell in Scotland the division was moved to Liverpool.

I took a deep draught of beer and thought for a little while about Liverpool. It was there that I had had my first real experience of air-raids. I remembered the initial fascination of trying to see what was going on—a fascination which did not last long. I remembered the nights of duty at the docks, on those frequent occasions when the troops were called in, the burning timber, the tumbling warehouses.

I remembered, too, that it was from Liverpool that I was first sent for an interview for a commission. I had to report to some department in Northumberland Avenue at 11.15 hours one morning. The train on which I travelled down from Liverpool was delayed, held up in an air-raid, and I reached London with only a few minutes to reach my goal. With the help of a friendly taximan I just managed it, filled up a large form and settled down to wait. I had had nothing to eat since five o'clock the previous evening.

All sorts of civilians were called for, till finally, at a quarter to two, the door opened and a voice said: "Lance-corporal McDougall!" I sprang to my feet, marched into the room and saluted a red-tabbed figure who was sitting at a table, holding in his hand the form I had filled in. He took a long time looking me over, and I waited, standing rigidly to attention. At last he spoke.

"You state here," he said, "that you studied at the University of Greifswald in Germany."

"Yessir," I said.

He flipped the question form disdainfully on to the table, and said in bored accents: "I've never heard of it."

For a moment I stood at a loss. Then I said reasonably: "That's scarcely my fault, is it, sir?"

This only served to annoy him, however, and he said sharply: "It's no use, Corporal. You must realize that we have on our waiting list men better fitted for this type of work, men with good degrees. . . ." At that point, to coin a phrase, something snapped. The Scots are notoriously touchy on any matters relating to education, and I flared up at once. The last thing I heard the idiot say as I was ejected was: ". . . and what is more, I'll see to it that you *never* hold a commission!"

The memory of the expression on the face of the

spluttering officer made me laugh aloud as I finished up my beer. A thickset Pole looked at me in amazement and made some unintelligible comment to his companions. I looked again all round the bar. Nobody I knew had come in. Edinburgh seemed empty of my friends. I ordered another pint and returned to my reminiscing.

From Liverpool the division moved in the spring of 1941 to Ireland, where the only highlight as far as I was concerned was the fact that, after playing for a civilian cricket club throughout the summer, I was picked for a Northern Irish select eleven and played against Hedley Verity.

It was in the summer of 1941 that I first heard of Commando units at all, and began to put in applications for a move. I was by then a sergeant, and when I discovered that my section officer, thinking that I was simply tired of the monotony of the life, had been tearing up my applications, I filled in a form of application for a commission, got him to sign it and took it round to Div. H.Q. myself.

Thereafter began the long series of boards and interviews, which finally resulted in my being sent to Pre-O.C.T.U. and thence, in March, 1942, to O.C.T.U. at Dunbar. In answer to my request the Company Commander told me that I might get a recommendation for Commando work, but I could not be posted direct to a Commando unit. I played rugby till the end of the season, then I played cricket and tennis for the O.C.T.U. I passed out an "A" cadet—and was posted straight back to the Intelligence Corps.

At the Corps depot at Oxford I was interviewed by the Commandant, a kindly man, who seemed genuinely concerned on hearing that I did not want to be an intelligence officer with a division.

"You'd best do the courses with the others anyway," he said. "Then we shall see how you feel about things."

I knew that if I once did the courses I was doomed. I made a deliberate hash of the first one, collected my rocket for it and was sent before the Commandant, who twinkled benignly at me and said: "You'd better try Matlock."

The course at Matlock was a six weeks' one on Staff Duties and War Intelligence. I found an American-Swede, and a Canadian, and a club with vast supplies of draught beer and at least enjoyed the evenings.

From Edinburgh I sent a silent toast to Carlsson and little Wink Johnson wherever they might now be. They had been good company.

But when I had returned to Oxford with another damning report I had found myself almost permanent Orderly Officer until the next course, one of Interrogation, at Cambridge. This time, in spite of myself, I enjoyed the course. It was the first time I had used German since leaving the University more than three years previously, and I liked it. I was sent on from there to London to spend some time doing interrogation in a prisoner-of-war cage, and there I had my first real stroke of luck. I met a man who had been with No. 2 Commando at Vaagso as intelligence officer. He came up to me one evening and said casually: "I hear you want to get to a Commando unit."

At once I was all agog.

"Well," he said, "I know that No. 4 are short of one or two officers, and I might be able to wangle you an interview. Then it's up to yourself."

I was profuse in my thanks.

"There's just one thing," he went on. "When you go back to the depot now, don't let yourself be posted whatever you do, until you hear from me, which should be in a couple of weeks."

I returned to the depot, wondering how the hell I was going to stop my posting. All the courses were now finished; I was bound to be sent to a division very shortly.

Then I had my second stroke of luck. I was alone in the bar, wondering what I should do about things, when the Adjutant, a grey-haired little man from the last war, came in. We had a drink together and in the course of conversation I learned that he had known my uncle in the Cameron Highlanders in the last war, and had been one of the very few surviving officers at Loos where my uncle had been killed. I plied him with drink, and as we grew more and more convivial I told him of my problem.

"Leave it to me!" he cried. "I'll arrange everything. Can you sing any of the songs your uncle used to sing?"

My uncle was killed about two years before I was born, so I didn't know, but as the evening wore on it didn't seem to matter, and we parted on very good terms indeed.

For the next two weeks I kept out of everybody's way, and on the odd occasions when I saw the Adjutant he laid one finger on the side of his nose and gave a conspiratorial wink. All apparently was well.

By the middle of the third week, however, he was wearing a rather worried frown, and stopped me as I made my furtive way to lunch.

"Look here," he said. "You'll have to do something about this business. I've torn up three separate letters about you in the last few days, and sooner or later they'll be 'phoning the Commandant."

I sent a frantic wire to the man in London, only to receive the answer: "You should hear any day now." At the end of the week it came, a letter inviting me to go to Winchester, to be interviewed by Lord Lovat, then commanding No. 4 Commando. On the following Tuesday I went, in a fever of excitement. After several questions about my age, fitness and various activities, Lord Lovat said thoughtfully: "The trouble is, this post of intelligence officer is more or less booked, and the only other vacancy we have at the moment is as a section officer with an assault troop." He seemed quite startled when I burst out: "But I don't want to be I.O.," and went on to tell him the whole story. At the end of the recital he said, non-committally: "Hm, well we'll see. I'll let you know in the next few days." The interview was at an end.

Back at Oxford the Adjutant eyed me with a sceptic eye. Four more days elapsed. Then came a letter with the Winchester postmark. It told me that if I were still of the same mind I was to report to the headquarters of the Commando on 18 December. I would then be sent to "F" troop, to which, after the unit had been on Christmas leave, I would be attached on a month's probation. Whether I stayed with the unit after that would depend upon how I acquitted myself during the probationary period.

I rushed to the Adjutant.

"Thank God for that!" he said. "Now here's a leave pass. Get out of here and go away somewhere till you report to Winchester. I'll write these people and tell them you're no longer here."

I required no second telling, thanked him and disappeared. I was never back.

Now as I stood up to catch the barman's eye in the crowded bar in Edinburgh I wondered how the others were getting on. Len would probably be out at that pub outside Newcastle where he and Jill generally spent part of their leave, while Peter would be rushing around London. I surveyed the milling throng of strangers all around me and listened to the confusion of language and dialect. I longed for the sight of a known face, but my friends were by now either dead or prisoners or overseas. They certainly didn't seem to be at home. I had never known a great many girls before the war, though I had met vast numbers of them at University hops and so on, but even the girls I had known were now either married or engaged or in one or other of the services. I was a stranger in my own town.

CHAPTER II

The lyf so short, the craft so long to lerne
Th' assay so hard, so sharp the conquering.
CHAUCER: *Parlament of Foules*

WHEN I had joined "F" troop, to replace John MacDonald, who had been killed at Dieppe, each troop had been engaged on individual training. That meant I did not come in contact with the members of other troops very often. I had felt very inadequate as I set out day after day to take my section on some form or other of battle training. After all, most of them had been in action quite recently and knew more about the practical side of the thing than I did. So I confined myself as far as possible to field training and to route marches, which I knew I could do as well as most. On one of these we had passed a section from another troop with their officer, a strong-looking character with black hair and a magnificently broken nose. After passing the time of day with him, and arranging to meet him that evening for a drink, we went our several ways.

Marching along beside the Sergeant-major in front of the whistling troop I asked him the officer's name, which I had missed in our conversation.

"That's Mr. Coulson, sir," said the C.S.M.

"An' a bloody good officer an' all," put in the voice of his bosom companion, McVeigh, immediately behind us, "ain't 'e, Taff?"

"Ar, 'e is," the C.S.M. had agreed.

I had been interested, when first I joined No. 4, to find out what they were all like, these men I had read about in the Press. They had been written up in so many different ways that many of the other Army units were doubtful as to whether they were super-efficient soldiers or hoodlums let loose. Few even knew the formation of the unit.

I discovered that there were altogether about 435 all ranks in each separate Commando, six troops of three officers and sixty, with H.Q. troop, which included the medical section and signals section, making up the remainder. This establishment was by then more or less fixed in all the different Commando units, although any one unit could be adapted at short notice to meet the requirements of any particular task, as had happened, for example, when No. 2 Commando had used most of the R.E. personnel from various Commandos for their operation at St. Nazaire.

Apparently the whole idea for such an irregular force had been born in the mind of Colonel Dudley Clark, who in the summer of 1940 was assisting the C.I.G.S., Sir John Dill. The Navy was fit to fight, the R.A.F. was fit to fight, but the Army was in bad shape. Morale after the evacuation from France was not high, equipment was lacking, and certainly no major force could be fitted out for some considerable time. Why not then have a small striking force, trained, mobile, swift, aggressive, which could be taken by ship to any part of the huge coastline held by the enemy, land, destroy and depart, like the Norsemen of old?

His idea was welcomed by the C.I.G.S. and the Prime Minister, and on 9 June, 1940, an appeal for volunteers was circulated round each Command. No details were given in this appeal as to the exact nature of the work, but the special service was to be fighting duties only. Each volunteer would have the option of returning to his own unit after having been interviewed and told of the tasks he would be required to perform.

After only two months, however, this appeal, in spite of the powerful support it had from its instigators, met with considerable opposition from the Regular departments of the War Office. This opposition group viewed with alarm and marked hostility the growth of a body of troops, completely independent, answerable to only three or four people in the know, and apparently under the hand of the Prime Minister. It was revolutionary, and as such had to be condemned. When Admiral Sir Roger Keyes was appointed

Director of Combined Operations he found, at the beginning of August, 1940, that he was face to face with defeat before the band of volunteers had so much as struck a blow. To appease the War Office, the Independent Companies which already existed were amalgamated with the new formations to form one cumbersome and unwieldy Special Service Brigade. This did not last long, and at the beginning of 1941 was re-grouped as separate Commandos again.

In March, 1941, No. 4 Commando took part in the raid on Lofoten, a happy-go-lucky affair in which the only casualty was an officer whose pistol, which he was carrying in his pocket, went off and shot him in the leg. Although there was not a great deal accomplished in the raid, it did catch the imagination of the public, and did serve to justify the existence of Commando units in the eyes of their supporters.

Within the Commando itself there were very real difficulties to be overcome. To start with, everyone had joined the Commando from different units, with different equipment and with totally different ideas on warfare. Unit equipment was in extremely short supply, especially signals equipment, which was almost wholly lacking. Wireless communication was simply non-existent and inter-troop communication consisted of a complicated system of bird-whistles. Tommy-guns were issued out before an operation from a central pool and were withdrawn again as soon as the operation was over.

As can be imagined in such a haphazard organization, characters emerged and personalities very quickly came to the fore. The nucleus of the real No. 4 Commando was already there.

After Lofoten the unit trained along lines designed to keep everyone at a peak fitness. There were pack marches, load-carrying marches, speed marches, cross-country marches and cross-country runs. Any man who fell out of one of these was sent out the next day on a "remedial" parade, to do the thing again. An officer was not allowed to fall out.

The result of this type of training was the growth of a tremendous troop spirit, as the training was carried out by troops, and the stronger members helped the weaker brethren along and each would share the load of the next man. That meant the unit was no longer simply a number of separate individuals, but a number of groups, each group being a troop. And all the time the process of sorting and weeding-out was going on. The Press had given the unfortunate impression that a Commando unit was a collection of thugs and street-corner boys whose best weapon would have been a razor or a jagged bottle, but it had been found very early on that this type was no use to the unit, as such a man did not take kindly to teamwork or to discipline, and these were of necessity the basis of all Commando work.

The next major operation undertaken by the unit was a landing near Boulogne in April, 1942, where a fairly long patrol was carried out without loss. Again little was achieved from the purely military point of view, but each successful landing served to increase the confidence of the troops concerned in their ability to work as a team. Every operation carried out by any Commando helped towards the success of the next raid, because all experience was pooled and faults in technique could thus be studied and remedied.

At the War Office, Sir Roger Keyes had been succeeded by Lord Louis Mountbatten as Chief of Combined Operations. Sir Roger Keyes had had a hard row to hoe and spoke in the House of Commons of his disappointments and frustration. He had in his term of office, however, stood manfully by his task, and had seen the Commando units justify themselves sufficiently to prevent their being thrust into the background by the zealous and extremely jealous staff-officers, who had devoted the greater part of their lives to the training and production along standardized lines of efficient and well-disciplined Regular soldiers. The opposition put up by these conventionalists was stubborn and enduring; it lasted until the ultimate disbanding of all Commando units in 1946, when the dust of Whitehall was disturbed by a long sigh of relief.

As I sat remembering all this I thought of the regular soldiers who had been in the Commando when I joined it. Of the officers about one-third were Regulars, first-class as officers and also as men, which in a Commando unit was just as important, since they came in much closer contact with the troops under their command than they would have done in an ordinary unit.

The Commando was essentially an infantry assault unit, but there were as many as eighty-five different units of the Army represented in it at one time. Pay day was a nightmare of acquittance rolls for the H.Q. staff, as there had to be a separate roll for every regiment which had a man there. Curiously enough, the regiment with the greatest number of men represented was the Royal Artillery, whose members are not normally noted for their fondness for foot-slogging.

Marching had been the main pastime of the Commando when I did my month's probation period, and it was on these marches that I first came to know the troop and the personalities in it. We used to march out some distance from the town to a suitable training area where we were to try out some form of battle-drill, or do field-firing or simply weapon-training, since there had recently been a new intake of men.

At first I had been disconcerted by the fact that, while I was running over the battle-drill we had to try out, there was a certain scepticism in the way they were listening. I looked round the faces of the audience till I met the gaze of a small, black-haired, square-jawed man, whose beady black eyes seemed to gleam out from under craggy black brows. His whole demeanour was so seriously unbelieving that I grinned at him and said: "Well, what's wrong with it?"

The black eyes lit up as he grinned in return.

"It jus' won't work, sir. These things never work. They're jus' something someone's put down on paper because it looks good an' it'll get him promotion. The man that works them things out never 'as to use 'em."

30

Being new, I had tried to reason with him.

"But it seems all right, doesn't it? There's no reason why it shouldn't work." Again he had shaken his head.

"Look, sir. It don't make any difference wot they call 'em, there's still only one way to do the job these drills are supposed to do for you, an' that's by fire an' movement. Bags of fire an' bags of movement. Drills are all right when you're trainin' with the General watchin', but in action, when things are never wot you expect, you soon forget all the drills an' stick to fire an' movement."

"Well," I said, "surely that's a drill itself!"

"Ar," he grinned. "Well, let's cut out the fancy stuff an' get back to it!"

That was my first defeat by McVeigh, who in the times to come was to prove a tower of strength in the troop. Small in stature, slimly built, his personality was such that he became an almost legendary figure throughout the whole Commando.

It was from the Sergeant-major that I learned most about McVeigh, for they were a pair who had soldiered together for years in the same battalion of the Loyal Regiment, and who had stuck together ever since through thick and thin. "You want to see 'im box," said the C.S.M. "Marvellous 'e is. Runner-up at 'is weight in the 'ole Army 'fore the war." He grinned reminiscently. "'E kept us in beer-money for long enough when we was in Shanghai."

"How?" I asked.

"Well, we was on'y privates like an' never seemed to 'ave no money see, an' it was always easy to fix up a fight for some cup or other, so I used to arrange the fight, an' when 'e won, I'd flog the cup for beer-money see? That an' the money we made bettin' on 'im kept us goin'."

"What happened when he got beaten?"

"We was up the creek," said the Sergeant-major simply. "But that didn't often 'appen, 'e was a luvly fighter, was McVeigh."

"And have you been together ever since?"

"Well, we 'ad a spell on the Reserve, near killed us it did.

McVeigh was a postman an' walked miles. When war began we was back in."

"How did you get here?"

"Well, we 'ad a 'ell of a doin' at Dunkirk. You know, gettin' positions all ready facin' one way, then 'avin to leave 'em, or 'avin the Germans comin' in the other way. Nobody told us nothin', an' goin' back all the time without a chance to do any fightin', an' them Stukas all the time. Well, we 'finished up back in the depot. I never saw a bloke as browned-off as McVeigh. Desprit, 'e was. Nothin' but boozin' an' bashin' the depot-wallahs, if we 'adn't got 'ere, we'd've been in clink soon enough. Then we went to Achnacarry, an' I took promotion but 'e wouldn't, an' so 'ere we are!"

"And you still go around together?"

"Ar, we share the same billet. Course on parade's on parade like, an' you'll never find a smarter soldier than McVeigh. I'll bet you never 'ave to peg *'im*, sir! An', sir, don't you take no notice of wot 'e says, 'e's always got to 'ave a moan, but 'e'll always back you up."

The Sergeant-major had then departed to chase up the laggards at the back of the troop, and I had continued the march with my section sergeant at my side. This was Eric Cross, who had been with the unit since the first, and who later became its best Administration Officer. Eric was a quiet-spoken pipe-smoker who always gave the impression of taking a reflective puff before committing himself to an answer. Unhurried and unflurried, he ministered most efficiently to the needs of the troop in his capacity of T.Q.M.S., while running his section just as efficiently in training.

From him I had a first-hand report of the action at Dieppe, where the Commando had registered the only complete success of the whole operation. The main assault had, of course, been made on the town itself by the Canadians, but there were two batteries, situated one on either side of the town, covering the seaward approaches.

No. 3 Commando had been given the task of dealing

with the battery on the left, and No. 4 that on the right. On the way across, the landing-craft of No. 3 Commando had been unfortunate enough to run up against a number of enemy vessels about eight miles off the French coast. They were at once engaged in a sea battle in which the crowded little landing-craft had little or no chance of success. They suffered very heavy casualties in this action as they pressed on towards the coast, so that their force when they landed was so small that they were not able effectively to deal with the battery, whose crews had already been aroused by the sounds of battle off shore.

Over on the right, however, No. 4 was more fortunate and made their landfall at exactly the right place just at dawn.

"Didn't you see anything at all of the ships that No. 3 ran into?" I asked.

"We could see the tracer over the left," said Eric Cross. "But we didn't see any ships."

"What happened when you all got ashore?" I then asked.

"The unit was split into two main groups," said Eric, "and the first one under the second-in-command, Major Mills-Roberts, had to engage the battery from the front, while the other under the C.O., Lord Lovat, went inland to take it from the rear. We were lucky at the beginning, when 'C' troop, who had to make their way up a gully filled with wire, blew the lot up with a Bangalore torpedo. It went off just when a flight of Spitfires were thrashing across overhead and they drowned the noise of the bang. Then the whole of the other party followed 'C' troop up the cliff, while we pushed on the other way.

"When we got to a wood behind the battery position we formed up for the attack, with 'F' troop on the one side and 'B' troop on the other. We could hear 'C' troop mortars firing into the battery, and one bomb landed on a pile of charges. The whole lot went up. We began to move forward from the wood towards a little farm-building, and when we reached it we saw a gang of Germans in the yard forming up to counter-attack 'C' troop. The tommy-gunners killed the lot of them, but as we came past the building we had to cross an open space before the wire of the battery itself. That was where Captain Pettiward got killed. When he went down Mr. Macdonald ran forward and he was hit too, and died before we got back to the beach. That left the troop without an officer, and as the C.S.M. had been wounded already...."

"The Sergeant-major we have now?"

"No, Taff Edwards has taken over the troop since then. This was a chap called Stockdale. Well, he had been wounded, and things were a bit muddled, and that was when Captain Porteous got his V.C. He was keeping contact between 'B' troop and ourselves, and when he saw how things were with us he ran in and got us organized. He was wounded, too, at that time. Not badly, but shot in the hand by a German at close range. He grabbed the German's bayonet and stabbed him with it and led the rush at the gunpits. The whole troop went through them after him and he was wounded again as he reached the last gunpit. All the guns were destroyed and any Germans left were sorted out, and we ran up a Union Jack over the position, and laid out the chaps who had been killed just under it. We were really very lucky—we had only nine killed and about forty-five wounded." He laughed. "Did you know we had Yanks with us too?"

"No, I didn't know that."

"Well, we had. There was a chap called Koons, who was the first American of the war to get a British gong—he got an M.M.—and the other chap, I can't remember what his name was, got bitten by a horse as we went through the farmyard and went home and got the Order of the Purple Heart."

"What for?"

"Wounded in action!"

Eric always swore by this tale of the American, and I laughed to myself as I remembered it.

I stood up to try and catch the barman's eye and as I did

so was hailed by a figure struggling through the throng around the bar.

"Mac! What are you doing here? How long are you home for?"

It was a long time since I had seen George, who was in the uniform of the Fleet Air Arm.

"I've still got about five days, what about you?"

"Well, I've to go before a board tomorrow, and if I'm fit I go back after that. I made a coddy of a landing and burst my shoulder."

"Ah well, here's to the board, George; you keen to get back?"

George looked apologetic. "Well, I've been home quite a while, and you keep seeing chaps for a couple of days, then they disappear again, and you feel a bit of a chancer hanging about on your own with all this mob." He waved an expressive hand at the crowded bar. Then he looked at me. I was in civilian clothes.

"What are you doing now, Mac? You were in Intelligence or something weren't you?"

"That's right, clever chap, me. I got to a Commando unit just over a year ago now, at the end of 1942; but don't get any wrong ideas, I've done a lot of walking since I got to them and not much else."

George looked doubtful.

"What possessed you to join them? Do you get stacks of danger money or something?"

"Well, there's always the billeting allowance. I suppose you might call that danger money in some cases."

"Do you not get extra pay, though?"

"No, you don't get any extra, but there's a lot of other things that make it well worth while. I think I'm damn lucky that they'll have me."

The barman called time, we drank up and left the heat of the pub and went into the cool air outside. George fled for a bus with a shouted farewell and I turned my steps towards Princes Street. I decided to walk the three miles home. The town was dark under the black-out, but the outline of the Castle stood out clearly against the cold sky as I headed westward.

My thoughts were still with the unit as I walked. I had not found any group of supermen when I had joined, but a lot of ordinary decent men of all shapes and sizes whose only common factor was a desire to do something in the war, to take a personal part in it. Some were undoubtedly fired by a feeling of patriotism or high ideals, but most were inspired by a much less articulate desire than that—perhaps an innate dislike of the shirker—maybe an urge to escape from the routine of a searchlight site or infantry battalion. Whatever the cause, the result was a unit that, after the operation at Dieppe, was at its peak, fit, confident and well-disciplined.

Most of the men in the troops as private soldiers had been N.C.O.s in their own units and had voluntarily given up rank to be allowed to join the Commando, and while this may have meant a financial loss to them as individuals, it was certainly the unit's gain, since these men were capable of taking over a sub-section or a section if need be at a moment's notice.

Every man in the Commando enjoyed the luxury of a civilian billet, for which he was given an allowance of six shillings and eightpence a day. There were usually two men to each billet, and when the day's parades were over they were free—although on call at two hours' notice—until the following parade next morning. This civilian billet arrangement made soldiering a pleasure. It meant so many things to us all. After tearing round some assault course somewhere you could have a bath. Each day you could eat from a table with a cloth on it. You felt human. And how well most of the landladies looked after the troops billeted on them!

I had wondered about the training in a unit such as the Commando, but when I took part in it I found that although it was strenuous at times and realistic at all times, particularly on any sort of field-firing exercise where live ammunition was always used, it was all obviously directed towards a specific purpose, and because it had some point and bearing on the war most of the troops enjoyed it.

For the most part each troop trained separately, sending in a training programme each week to H.Q. for approval. Most mornings were spent in weapon training of some sort, and the afternoons in map and compass exercises round the countryside. Each week we had one route march of fifteen to twenty miles and sometimes a cross-country run, while once in three weeks or so we had a Commando exercise which usually meant a march of about twenty-five miles out, a fairly unpleasant night scheme, then a march of twenty-five miles back the next day.

Sometimes this Commando scheme was designed to harass some particular branch of H.Q., in which case the troops of the Commando sent out only their H.Q.s on the exercise. These sent in frequent messages and situation reports, if the butt of the exercise was the signals section or the Intelligence section, who tried frenziedly to cope with the flow of messages and information sent in.

Fairly infrequently there would be an exercise on a bigger scale, taking in the whole Brigade, and designed to test everyone from the Brigadier down. These larger exercises were not the happy-go-lucky day-out-with-the-boys affairs we enjoyed in the Troops; they were grim, ponderous and intricate inventions in which masses of troops marched fantastic distances, only to lose contact with everyone else; rations and supplies were sent off into the blue to some mysterious rendezvous and never turned up until the finish of the whole show; nights were spent in stumbling along winding lanes jammed with transport going the other way, then in plodding across country, with the conviction growing in every man's mind that the chap at the front was completely lost; wireless contact would be established long enough to pick up snatches of messages which were the more confusing by being out of context; on one occasion the transport sent out to pick up a certain band of warriors in the night picked up the wrong ones and bore them, surprised and contented, away, while the enraged Signals personnel of the original lot sent livid messages hurtling to and fro across the ether, and the troops in the ditches round about blasphemed.

After I had been with the unit a couple of months "F" troop went off "on Commando" to Falmouth. This meant that the troop moved away from the rest of the unit and spent a fortnight doing independent training in a different area. The area was selected by the Troop commander, ostensibly for its training facilities, but more frequently for some slightly less military motive. In any case, it was a good thing to get right away from H.Q. for a while and to have some variety in the routine of the troop. It also meant that the troop was entirely responsible for its own administration and rationing. As a rule a seaside town was chosen, so that landing training could be carried out and trips on mine-sweepers and M.T.B.s fixed up. On such an excursion "C" troop, under David Style, generally went to some area like St. Ives, where they could practise climbing, scaling and ropework, because they were the specialist troop in that sort of thing.

We had gone down to Falmouth, however, in the month of February and spent the mornings happily enough, swimming when it was warm enough to do so, and sending each sub-section of men out to reconnoitre the area for the exercises we were planning for the rest of the time. Most of the afternoons we spent playing football or doing a ten-to-fifteen-mile march. One day we decided to have a longer march from Falmouth to Truro to Redruth and back to Falmouth. We were to carry packs filled with bricks to represent explosive. Before setting out I went round the troop checking the weight of the various packs. I came to the stocky figure of old Donkin, the oldest man in the troop, who disliked marching as much as did McVeigh.

"How much weight have you got there, Donkin?" I asked him. He looked up at me.

"Oh reckon ah've as much as you 'ave, sir," he said with his Durham burr. As my batman had filled my pack in view of the troop I could scarcely stagger, and I could not believe that Donkin would himself fill his pack with such a load. I went round behind him.

"I'll just give it a lift and see," I said. Then I heaved at the pack in front of me, which seemed to weigh a ton, while Donkin gave the appropriate grunts as I let go. It certainly did not lift easily.

We set out along the hard and flinty Cornish roads. Sweat ran down in rivulets and the pack-straps cut into raw shoulders. After eighteen miles we dumped the bricks that weighed us down and turned for home. Donkin was comparatively fresh, and I noticed that his pack did not look empty like the others. At the next halt I went up to him.

"Let's have a look at that pack of yours," I said, going round to open it.

A slow grin broke over the craggy face. He sighed. "Well," he said, "at least ah've watched you sweat, sir." His pack was filled with empty tins wrapped in paper, and his pack was tied to his belt, so that I would be lifting him when I tested the weight of the pack. I glanced round the troop. Toombs had an anti-tank rifle. "Here, Toombs," I said. "Give Donkin a shot of that anti-tank, you can take his rifle if you like."

We started off again, Donkin plodding along beside me. He looked round under the length of the Boyes rifle. "Shall ah tell you 'bout the loads we carried w'en ah was a young soldier?" he asked, then gave a gust of Rabelaisian laughter. A man of character was Donkin.

The roads round the Falmouth area had such an effect on the feet that when the whole unit moved to that district in March, 1943, we carried out an exercise called "Sorefeet," which consisted of an outward march of some thirty-odd miles, followed by a ghastly night scheme in pouring rain, then the march back on the following day, which was hot and dry. The effect on the sodden feet was excruciating. Mile succeeded burning, blistering mile until we reached a point some five miles from home, where we were marched into a field to be inspected by Someone from Group.

"F" troop, enjoying the reputation it had earned itself

39

for being the best marching troop of the Commando, stood at ease on its simmering soles and watched with almost hysterical mirth the less fortunate trying to stamp briskly to attention before the inspecting officer. The crowning moment came when troop after troop made its way on to the hard high road and winced its way past on tiptoe giving an agonized "Eyes Left."

It was from Falmouth, too, that we had carried out the exercise known as "Brandyball" at St. Ives. The purpose of the exercise was to prove that a force of men could be landed by the Navy on a shore so rocky that it would be undefended. There were many such fronts on the coasts of enemy-occupied territory, just as there were on our own. If such a landing could be achieved it might be possible to put ashore a Commando brigade on a suitable spot in France. The brigade could then attack and clear a port from the landward side, to hold it until the main force could make its landing in the port itself.

Near St. Ives rocky cliffs rise sheer from the Atlantic surf to a height of some four hundred feet, then flatten on to a scrub-covered plateau on the top, criss-crossed by stone dykes. David Style, whose troop knew the area well, was placed in charge of the initial training, which consisted of successfully getting up and down the rocky cliffs.

We began from the top, and the first task was to get everyone down to the foot, which was no easy business. As we gazed timidly from the cliff-top into the seething surf far below I heard one man ask his neighbour: "Wot's them little white things dahn there?" and the laconic reply: "Seagulls."

Going down a cliff always seems worse than climbing up. The steadiest head can be assailed by giddiness, the surest foot can slip and the sight of the whirling surf below was not at all an attractive one. We finally reached the bottom without mishap, however, and I for one was overcome with relief at not having been dizzy on the way down. I looked up at the mass of rock above me and was horrified to find that the clouds scudding across the towering crags above gave the impression that the whole mass was swaying forwards, so that I began to sway backwards, towards the hissing water behind me.

Once down it was necessary to climb up again, another task which brought its own particular problems, and when that was done the whole process was repeated. Throughout this awkward clambering up and down old Donkin and McVeigh, the best climbers in the troop, were invaluable. I found it strange that two old soldiers, who generally disliked exercise on principle, so obviously enjoyed this sort of thing. They went up and down the cliff face as though they were crossing the street, while the rest of us clung convulsively to one handhold, then another. Later we did the ascent and descent in groups and subsections, the formations in which we would be on landing, and finally we carried weapons and ammunition and practised till that part of the training was complete.

Then came the shattering news that the Navy, holding the view that to land anywhere on such a coast was impossible, had refused to risk their craft and would therefore send none. The C.O., Lord Lovat, then sent for some Goatley boats, which are collapsible, flat-bottomed things operated by about a dozen men kneeling and wielding the paddles. They are normally used in river and canal crossings.

On the final rehearsal, the night before the exercise proper, we all embarked at St. Ives in tank landing-craft with the Goatley boats on board. There was an eighteen-foot swell on the Atlantic, which rolled and slumped rather unpleasantly against the foot of the cliff face.

It was very difficult to launch the craft into the water from the L.C.T.s,* but it was finally accomplished without anyone having to swim for it, and the Goatley boats began their slow, tortuous journey towards the cliffs. They were certainly not the craft one would choose of one's own accord. At times the paddle-blades were completely submerged, at times they struck wildly at air, so heavy was the swell. The

* Landing Craft Tank.

Navy had thoughtfully provided a rescue launch, which stayed about three hundred yards out. The surf at the rock base was terrifying in aspect, and when the first man leapt ashore on the left-hand landing place with the rope to secure the craft, he slipped, the craft was whisked out by the receding wave, thrown in the air and overturned. In spite of all the efforts of David Style and David Haig-Thomas, two men were never seen again.

The rest of us were ordered back to the L.C.T.s and the remainder of the trial was cancelled. Next day the swell had abated somewhat and the demonstration was completed without further mishap; we landed, scaled the cliffs, paused for a moment below the crest to regain some breath, then stormed over into the assault of a mock position a little way inland. The War Office V.I.P.s looked on impassively and only the Naval officers seemed impressed.

After a few more weeks in Falmouth, pleasantly enough spent, we moved north to Braemar, where for some six weeks we never did a day's training without first having to climb a thousand feet. We stormed down from our various camps in the hills each week-end like packs of wolves, till, on a sudden flap, we were rushed off to Troon, where the unit had been billeted in the early days, filled with the rumour that we were going overseas.

But in August, 1943, we moved instead to the south coast. The troops were in different towns in Sussex, with H.Q. in Seaford, along with "A" and "B" troops, "C" and "D" troops were in Newhaven, while "E" and "F" were as far away as possible in Lewes. I had been in charge of the advance party as billeting officer.

It was here that the whole unit fell into a period of depression. The troops were browned-off, they were fitter than they had ever been before, confident and ready for action. It was a whole year since Dieppe, and men began to apply for posting back to their own units, many of which had been sent overseas in the meantime. These men pointed out that they had come to the Commando for action, and as McVeigh bitterly put it: "I've seen more action

comin' out of a pub on a Saturday night than I get in this
lot!"

Fortunately the unit was split up and sent off all over
the place on training in different parts of the country, which
kept us all so busy that there was little time for brooding.
"F" troop spent a week or two on the Norfolk Broads,
handling all sorts of craft from power boats down to rubber
dinghies. Then we joined the rest of the unit which had
forgathered at Brandon to train in forest fighting.

At Brandon the troop made the acquaintance of lion-
hearted little Admiral Sir Walter Cowan, who at the age
of about seventy-three had been retired for quite some time.
Somehow or other he had made himself into a sort of one-
man Commando, and in 1941 in the desert had been
captured by the Italians while engaging a tank with a re-
volver. The Italians had repatriated him after a time, and
now he turned up at Brandon to brush up his forest
technique.

The troops held him in great respect, which only increased when they heard his language. On one occasion he
was to be attached to my section in a night scheme, which
was to finish by a fairly long compass march through dense
woods back to the camp. Worried, I drew aside one, Guardsman Fraser of the Welsh Guards, and whispered in his ear:
"Look, Fraser. Your job on this whole thing is to keep an
eye on the Admiral. Give him a hand if he needs it, and for
God's sake don't lose him!"

We set off into the night, and the first part of the scheme
was uneventful. Then came the march back to the camp.
Each subsection plunged into the thick foliage of the woods
and disappeared. Inside the wood it was inky black. The
tree-tops were interlaced in such a way that it was impossible
to see the sky and stars. Branches whipped and scratched as
each man plunged on, desperately trying to keep contact
with the man in front. It seemed interminable.

At last, however, we reached camp, bursting forth from
the enveloping trees by some lucky chance right amongst
"F" troop lines.

43

There was a brew of scorching cocoa waiting, and as I stood trying to get the twigs and spikes out of my face and neck I was suddenly aware of Fraser standing by my side. I was seized by horrible doubt.

"Look 'ere, sir," he said. "I'm sorry, but I've lost the —— Admiral!"

"Who's lost the —— Admiral?" came a roar from behind us, and out of the trees stumbled a dishevelled little figure, indescribably dirty. "Let's have some of that —— cocoa!"

Some days later we returned to Lewes. By now Lord Lovat was Brigadier, Derek Mills-Roberts had some time previously taken command of No. 6, and so we were under command of Robert Dawson, who informed us when we assembled in H.Q. in Seaford that our role for the winter was to be small-scale raiding, carried out mainly from the dories, which would be taken to within striking distance of the enemy-held coast in M.T.B.s specially fitted with davits for the purpose. Pat Porteous was told that his troop, "D," would be the dory troop, and from time to time during the next few months he and the whole of his troop would disappear from our midst, to return some time later looking smug and revelling in the envy of the others.

In "F" troop we were condemned to spend a period of training in L.C.I.s,* which are singularly unattractive craft, capable of carrying about eighty men in acute discomfort. They have two ramps forward, one on either side of the bows, and these when let down invariably jut out above deck level, so that the leading man cracks his shins on the jutting end of the ramp and either hurtles down the thing on his hands and knees or falls headfirst into the drink, closely watched in either case by the sniggering sailor whose incompetence has been the initial cause of the mishap.

It was at this stage that Peter Mercer-Wilson gave up his post as Administrative Officer and came to us in the troop. Peter was a Regular officer in the R.A. and had been commissioned just about the beginning of the war. He was a

* Landing Craft Infantry.

44

conscientious type, and when he had been posted from Woolwich to a training regiment he had philosophically settled down to do his best until Fate in the form of the War Office posted him elsewhere. Then came the sinking of the *Royal Oak* at Scapa Flow, and Peter's young brother was one of those lost. The war became a personal thing then for Peter and without delay he wangled himself out of his own unit and into the newly-formed Commandos. By doing so he had undoubtedly jeopardized any chance of ultimate promotion in his own regiment, but he was prepared to take a chance on that.

The three of us shared the same billet in Lewes and it was from there that we set out for the period of training down at Warsash. There we reported for instructions, and were given the number of our L.C.I. for the duration of the training. On finding this craft we met its skipper, an appalling little man, who told us how lucky we were in being sent to his vessel. The whole of the first evening he told us this, and how he would have had his half-ring as Lieutenant-Commander if the Admiralty only knew their job. The troop took one look at him, heard him and christened him Nelson. Next day our training began.

The first day we wanted to do a few landings on a certain strip of shore, prior to doing a full-scale exercise there later. Nelson glanced at the map, assured us there was nothing easier, clanged bells, blew down whistles, bawled out the engineer, and we were seaborne. We missed that strip of shore by a good two miles in broad daylight, and when making the approach to the beach went in carrying far too much way, so that we eventually rammed the bows up the sloping shingle, and the ramps, that the idiot had had dangling out hopefully from the bows, now jutted up about five feet clear of the deck. We dropped ashore, thankful to get clear.

Once ashore we practised beach clearing for a time, then returned to the L.C.I., which was still where we had left it. We sat for about three hours waiting for the damn thing to float off, and when it did begin to move Nelson refused to allow us aboard until the whole ship was clear. Finally we had to wade out up to our necks and climb aboard. In the stuffy little cabin we sat listening to Nelson out on the bridge yelling orders at all and sundry and to the outspoken comments of the troop.

"What a day!" I said to Len and Peter. They nodded glumly, while Len with a worried look added: "And it's not finished yet." Peter and I looked at him questioningly.

"We've still got a night scheme to get through," said Len.

"Good God, if he's like this in the daytime what's he going to be like at night?"

Our worst fears were justified. Through some extraordinary blunder on the part of Nelson's cutter Peter and I were on board with the maps and the troop, while Len was on board some other ship with the details of the scheme when we set out. We ploughed through the darkness to some unknown destination, which Nelson eventually rammed at top speed, so that the leading man, who happened to be carrying McVeigh's Bren-gun, was thrown over the jutting end of the ramp into the water below. Once ashore we found Len, who told us we'd have to run, as the whole thing was already behind schedule. We were at the top of the beach, where there was a belt of double-apron wire. The night was inky black, and as we began to run along Len began to tell us the plan. We had gone about twelve paces when something caught my ankle and I felt flat on my face. Len waited impatiently till I got up, and we set out again. Another twelve paces or so and wham! Flat on my face again. When it happened for the third time, I struggled to my feet winded and furious, while Len, a yard or two out from me, was torn between exasperation and mirth, and McVeigh, just beyond him, forgetting the recent tragedy of his Bren, was slapping his thigh and crowing in hysterical glee: "E's done it again! 'Ark at 'im! It's as good as the pictures this is!"

After a nightmare cross-country run we reached the battery position, only to find that it was surrounded by a broad and evil-smelling moat. There was no way across, so the leading man took a rope over, which he made fast, and the rest of us swam through the foul water, with its clinging weeds, those men with Brens or mortars hanging on to the rope with one hand as they did so. The attack itself was an uninteresting affair, and after a short time we splodged wetly back to the L.C.I. and Nelson. Clambering back on board, we hoped our troubles were over. Not a bit of it. Grey fog descended on us as we returned towards Warsash, and Nelson in his wisdom decided to make fast to something. It was just our misfortune that the only thing he could find was a bell-buoy, which clanged its mournful dirge in our ears for the next five hours.

It was a weary troop that finally returned to Lewes the following day to try and rid ourselves of the foul smell of the moat and the chill of wet clothes. That evening we drank to Nelson's downfall and hoped we would never have the misfortune to be assigned to his craft for anything more than practice landings.

Next came the period of training for the troop operation from Dover, which culminated in disappointment and frustration, but which nevertheless had its moments of humour.

We had in the troop one member who was almost wholly night-blind. This fact had emerged at one of the tests to which we were from time to time subjected. We all had our night vision tested and it was found that several men were not as good as they might have been, while this one simply saw nothing. He was, however, a good soldier, and a keen one, and as a normal night is not entirely dark he was allowed to remain in the troop. It was then that we were ordered to Dover to carry out a troop-scale operation during the dark period of the month. This was a little awkward, and Len suggested to the man that it might be better if he did not take part in the operation. The poor chap was so disappointed that Len then decided to allow him to come on the boat, where he would remain with an anti-tank rifle with which he was to shoot out any searchlight that might catch us in its beam.

Happily the man went away and the training continued apace. We had made in the grounds of the huge desolate house in which we were immured a full-scale plan of the position we were due to attack, using wire where wire showed on the photographs, and marking in any known minefields on the route to the actual emplacements from the beach. We would take up our positions in the field, squatting down in the formations we would be in when in the boat, then on the order being given to land we swarmed out across the field, up a little bank to the first of the wire, and so on till we reached the huge mass of wire representing the enemy position. In the meantime the night-blind member stayed where he was in the field, timing our progress as we cut wire at the initial stage, made for the enemy wire, blew it up, cleared the position and returned realistically carrying our "casualties" to the boat.

One day, however, we were visited by a Brigadier from the War Office, who had heard of Commandos but wanted to see one or two. He watched the men form up in the field, followed us all round the course, returned to find the night-blind member lying contentedly in the winter sunshine.

"What," asked the Brigadier, "is this man doing?"

"Well, sir," said Len, "there is known to be a searchlight on the headland, and so we're having this man in the bows of the craft with an anti-tank rifle to shoot it out if it appears."

"Gad," said the Brigadier, impressed. "That's a good idea! But there's just one thing you've forgotten."

"Sir?" said Len politely.

"Yes, by gad," said the Brigadier. "That man will be dazzled by the light. He'll have to wear dark glasses!"

Len took a note and a pair of dark glasses were drawn for the benefit of the anti-tank rifleman.

One pastime frequently indulged in by the bored members of the troop was trying to catch the goldfish in a large ornamental pond in the middle of the lawn. Occasionally they varied this by trying to shoot the fish with a Colt automatic, but in neither pursuit did they succeed. One fish in particular attracted them. This was a huge lazy brute, obviously the king of the pond, which paid little or no heed to the enticing worms and other lures dangled so temptingly before it. This fish exasperated the troop, and when on Christmas night a party, led by Donkin, decided for once to make their way to the nearest pub, they stumbled forth into the blackness of the night as Donkin whispered hoarsely: "Ah know the way, ye can a' follow me."

They plunged across the lawn, there came a gargantuan splash, a moment's silence, then a volley of Durham oaths, punctuated by the gaspings and splutterings of the unfortunate Donkin as he floundered in the icy water. Nobody lifted a finger to help him. His friends stood listening in silent enjoyment. Then the dry voice of McCarthy broke the stillness from the edge of the pond: "Bring oot thon big yin, Harry."

After all the preparation, all the training and all the abortive attempts the operation had now been cancelled for good. We had scattered back to our various homes up and down the country to spend seven days recovering from the disillusionment. When we returned to Lewes after the leave it was early January. We began again on the old routine of marches, field-firing on the Sussex Downs and drinking beer in the evenings. Life seemed outwardly to be as before. One factor, however, had changed everything. The Second Front was in the air. There was talk of it in the Press, there was talk of it in the pubs. But the troop was still dispirited after the Dover affair, and it was McVeigh who caustically remarked:

"Open the Second Front? This lot couldn't open a can of bully!"

Nevertheless we felt the big stuff was coming our way, and this feeling was confirmed when the entire First Special Service Brigade, consisting of 3, 4 and 6 Commandos, and 45 Royal Marine Commando, was drawn up at Hove to be inspected by Montgomery. This was the first time that the whole Brigade had been on such a parade. The weather was bitterly cold, but Montgomery arrived punctually, made his inspection quickly, then called everybody round his jeep to address in his own curiously repetitive style.

The gist of his talk was that some time in the none too distant future the thing the newspapers called the Second Front would undoubtedly be opened. But not until he was good and ready. He never moved until he was good and ready, and this next move was going to be the decisive one, the one which would finally rout the German Army and finish the whole thing off. He praised the Brigade, some of whom had fought with him before, and he knew how to use us; we need have no fear. The mistakes of other campaigns would not be repeated. He looked to us to do a good job of work and he had every confidence that we would. It remained only for him to wish us good luck when the day of action came.

From then on training took a more definite shape. We were to practise infiltration schemes, "flat out" marches up to fifteen miles, then digging and defence schemes. There were to be seaborne exercises, landings and initial assaults. The whole Commando moved to Bexhill, where we could all be concentrated in the same town.

Every morning each troop started in battle order on a seven-mile sprint march to the training areas. That took fifty minutes. Once there, we formed up in operational order, i.e., by subsections, with H.Q. between the two sections, and began to march. On the march we crossed obstacles, attacked isolated haystacks and trees and worked out set battle-drills to meet various situations. After a break at midday we repeated the same sort of thing, except that senior ranks were gradually eliminated, the next senior taking over, until every man in the troop would, if necessary, take over command of the entire troop at a moment's notice.

The afternoon's march was always in the same direction —towards the assault course, over which we sweated, first of all by subsections, then as a troop, when on reaching the road we ran the last two and a half miles home. This last run was timed, and as a rule we managed it in about seventeen or eighteen minutes. By the time we reached the billets it was about half past five in the evening and the whole programme began again at 08.30 in the morning.

For the officers and N.C.O.s there were lectures on tactics and infiltration, which finally dragged to a close at about eight o'clock, by which time our muscles had stiffened and cramped to such an extent that all we were fit for was a couple of pints, a session with Peter's gramophone, then bed.

Peter Mercer-Wilson was one of the older inhabitants of the unit, though he was young in years. At first he had been with "B" troop, then after the raid at Boulogne he had become Administration officer, but had relinquished the third pip to come to "F" troop when he thought action seemed imminent. He had one section, I had the other, while we were both answerable to Len Coulson for our shortcomings.

Len himself hailed from Newcastle and was one of the strongest characters in the unit. He was not just physically big, although he had played for Northumberland as a wing forward before the war, but he was a Covenanter, a man of immense faith, without the desire to interfere with the affairs of others, though he was outspoken in the extreme in his defence of a principle. He had all the Northcountryman's respect for the Church, in which he frequently played the organ accompaniment, but he loathed hypocrisy in any form, as several padres attached to the unit discovered to their discomfiture. Yet for all his high standards, which he set more for himself than for others, he was not regarded as a man apart, for he had an earthy sense of reality which enabled him to meet and beat most men on their own ground. He could give a fluent dressing-down to any man in the troop any time he thought it necessary, while he could give just as fluent a rendering of "Blaydon Races" along with old Donkin at a troop "do" on a Saturday night.

Lord Lovat once said of him: "Order Len Coulson to do a thing he doesn't like and you'll have a hell of a time, but *ask* him to do the same thing and he'll work till he drops."

As he was the possessor both of a sense of humour and a wealth of common sense the Army and Len Coulson did not always see eye to eye, and as he was always ready to do battle on behalf of any member of the troop he was regarded with an apprehension almost amounting to dislike by various official bodies, who thought him quite unnecessarily "bolshie."

I always thought that Peter was frankly liked by the men in the troop. I was tolerated by the other section, defended by my own, but Len Coulson was held in absolute awe and respect by every man there. He was the rock on which the strength of the troop was built. As a member of the T.A. at the outbreak of war, Len had spent a bleak winter in a tent somewhere in Northumberland, then he had been commissioned in the Durham Light Infantry, and in 1941 had come to the Commando as a subaltern in "A" troop. Wherever we went the three of us shared a billet and stuck together through thick and thin. We grew to rely on one another in everything, and this stood us in good stead later on.

The breaking-in at Bexhill lasted about a fortnight and it was with some relief that we heard we were to do some seaborne training for the next while.

We went by train to Southampton, where one half of the unit embarked on H.M.S. *Princess Astrid* and the other half on the *Maid of Orleans*. These were the ships which were later to ferry us across on D-day. Each carried eight L.C.A.s* which, for any who are fortunate enough not to know, are low, flat-bottomed craft with an extremely shallow draught, which enables them to come very close inshore before the ramps forward are let down to enable the troops to run ashore dryshod. That at any rate is the theory, but dryshod is a comparative term and apparently covers any landing which does not include swimming.

It was unfortunate that these two ships, which were to

* Landing Craft Assault.

work in such close conjunction, should have been so different in atmosphere. On board the *Astrid,* with its R.N. and R.N.V.R. crew, all was well, but on the *Maid,* which was very soon rechristened, some were R.N.V.R., some were Merchant Navy, while some of the crew still seemed to be Southern Railway. As a result some were receiving "danger money," some were not, all were doing the same job, and the members of the Commando on board, living on pilchards and biscuits, felt as though they had interrupted a private feud, which indeed they had.

However, the two craft set out and began the long trip up to Cromarty Firth, where we were to carry out landing training along with an assault landing division. For the first few days at Cromarty we trained on our own, landing, marching, firing in remote spots and re-embarking again at the end of the day. Then for a week the weather was bad, so that the large-scale exercise had to be postponed, but finally we were swung outboard in the L.C.A.s into a grey heaving sea, while the cruiser *Berwick* fired overhead, and destroyers darted fairly close inshore, their guns twinkling. We landed behind the flails, which are tanks with an attachment jutting out forward. This consists of a revolving bar, held some six feet in front of the tank, and on this bar are innumerable chains which whirl round in a terrifying manner, striking the ground in front of the tank, and are intended to explode any mines which may be lurking there.

On leaving the beach we branched sharply left, to move as fast as possible through the dunes to the small town which was our objective. Here we were engaged by the local Home Guard, who fought with a fine disregard, common to most Home Guard, for all automatic weapons which had been dropped to give covering fire, but everyone seemed to enjoy the thing, and the admiring swarm of female spectators who thronged the streets were just as enthusiastic, blithely calling out advice and warnings to their menfolk, till we finally reached the "battery," when their hospitality was manifest to all, and cups of tea were handed out to the battle-stained warriors of both sides as fast as they could be filled.

This exercise was the last training of any importance that we undertook before returning to Bexhill to clean up and go on leave. It was now the beginning of April, 1944. When we returned from leave we were issued out with rucksacks of the Bergen type with a steel frame, and these were capable of holding a fantastic amount of kit. They had to. Every available thing which might be used in a fortnight, plus one hundred rounds of .303, one 3-in. mortar bomb, one pick and shovel and extra Bren magazines were crammed into the rucksack, which was then humped on to the back of the man who already had his equipment, bandolier and toggle rope draped on him, and who was carrying his rifle or tommy-gun. Every man carried about 90 lb. on his back.

In addition, some men had to carry pole charges, some Bangalore torpedoes, which are long metal tubes filled with explosive and used for blowing a gap in wire or for running into a pillbox. Some, instead of the rucksack, carried a smaller but just as heavy flamethrower. Medical orderlies were issued with a satchel containing medical kit, and carried a stretcher. All this was henceforth known as "operational order."

We were reinforced by the arrival of two French troops from No. 10 Inter-allied Commando, which now became part of the unit, so that our total strength was Commando H.Q., six British troops and two French troops, making a total of about six hundred men.

These six hundred men were to be seen almost every day staggering out in operational order on a ten-mile march "just to get used to it." Every man in the unit became heartily sick of the sight of the enormous rucksack which was now never unpacked, but lay overnight where it was dumped off raw shoulders to await the morning, when it would again be heaved up and borne away.

Gradually, in the midst of all this, we came to know various members of the French contingent, and to overcome the initial vague mistrust we had had of them as newcomers to the unit and to its standards. French troops as a rule are not good parade-ground troops by our standards, but these men certainly did their utmost to conform to what they must have felt were unnecessarily harsh regulations regarding dress, length of haircut, the angle of the beret, cleanliness of boots and belt and a host of other trivialities which beset them at every turn. In this matter of discipline and turn-out their officers went about very seriously the task of setting an example, and took great pains to find what was "done" and what was not.

Amongst the most serious of these officers was one Guy Vourch, whom I had already noticed when we were down near Folkestone on the abortive operation at Christmastime. Guy was a quiet, reserved young man with a thoughtful expression. He spoke excellent English and had a profound admiration for all things British. From him we heard a story typical of many a good Frenchman who had by some means or other made their way across from German-occupied France to carry on a private war from England. Guy was a member of a very old-established family in Brittany, where he was brought up. At the age of eighteen he left Finisterre for the first time to go to Paris to study medicine. It was there that the outbreak of war found him in 1939, and he was soon taken into the medical services of the French Army. Depressed by what he saw of the scramble for comfortable jobs, he applied for and was sent to an infantry O.C.T.U., where he was on the point of being commissioned when the collapse came. Everything and everyone seemed to be in confusion, and in the midst of all the turmoil the only clear order was that they should accept the armistice.

Guy was bewildered and disappointed. His world had fallen about him; it seemed that the glory of France was simply an echo from the past, the spirit of Verdun had hobbled out into the harsh light of reality and had there disintegrated. With this disillusionment came the hardening of resolve in the mind of the embittered Guy. England would carry on the fight, he must go there. There might still be a boat which could ferry him over, if he could only reach the coast. He set out at once for Rochefort, dodging enemy columns and making the fastest time he could, but he was too late. The last boat had gone. The Germans were hard on his heels, and entered the town before he could get away from it. He found himself a prisoner.

That night he escaped and made his way to Nantes, where he managed to change his uniform for civilian clothes. Then he boarded a train and returned to his own village of Plomodien in Finisterre. For the next month he tried to bribe any of the remaining fishermen to take him over to England, but was unsuccessful, and finally at the end of August he bought a 30-ft. fishing boat in need of repair, and set about preparing to take it across himself.

It was not until 21 October, 1940, that he was ready to undertake the crossing, with five others, among whom was his young brother Yves, who had been wounded in the fighting in May. They had sufficient food and water for about twenty-four hours. The engine gave out on the twenty-second, and they lay becalmed. This calm was followed by a gale from the north-east, which for four long days battered them south, only to be caught by a counter-blast from the south-west which almost spelled disaster. For another two days and nights they were driven along, at the mercy of the wind and sea, huddling together trying to survive in wet and cold, hunger and thirst. They now made no attempt at navigation, and had very nearly given up all hope when, on the thirty-first, ten whole days after leaving Douarnenez, they were at last picked up by S.S. *Cairngorm* somewhere off Milford Haven.

On reaching London all six joined the Free French Forces. Guy was sent to a camp at Camberley and commissioned. He then applied to be sent as an agent into France and did his parachute training to that end. The task for which he had been intended then lost its priority and he was attached for a year to the Political Intelligence Department in London. There was already in London quite a French colony, which had set up its own organization working independently of the British organization dealing with France, and Guy, openly distrustful of authority in any French form, began to apply to join the Commandos. He was posted to No. 10 Inter-allied Commando at the end of September, 1942, and had been with them ever since, until he came to us.

Of his people he had heard little at that time. He knew that his whole family was engaged in running one of the recognized underground channels of escape, under the code word "Johnny," and from time to time he heard through one of the escapers snatches of information about them. Now in Bexhill, he was concentrating every effort towards bringing himself and his troop to a peak of efficiency so that they might be the more effective when the time came.

May arrived. Training eased. We practised rapid movement through streets, over walls, through built-up areas, in which it is always difficult to maintain a steady rate of progress, as a sniper or machine-gun post can delay the leading troops, and those in the rear do not know the cause of the delay. They must obviously be warned, unless the obstacle is removed, so the leading troop commander has to make a snap decision as to whether or not the enemy post is sufficiently troublesome to merit an assault being made upon it, and, if not, how the rear troops are to be warned. Usually it is best to bypass the danger, and to leave a trail of tape or brightly coloured powder which can easily be followed over rubble.

So the inhabitants of Bexhill were at first amused and then not infrequently annoyed to see the Commando troops dashing along streets, then, for no apparent reason, swarming over walls, through deserted houses, across gardens, some cultivated, some deserted, then back on to the original axis of advance.

We made contact with the 6th Airborne Division, with whom we had previously done little or no training. At one time there had been some talk of the Commando being trained as paratroops, but this idea was later reduced to one troop, which was to be the Parachute troop, as any large-scale operation would naturally be carried out by the Airborne and only a small-scale job would come into the scope of the Commando itself. So "C" troop, under David Style, M.C., with Jack Wilson and David Haig-Thomas, did its jumps in the early part of 1944.

Now, however, we met the men of the actual Airborne Division at Bulford, where we stayed for a few days of inter-unit boxing and football. Between the various contests we were shown over the gliders and tug planes. Most of us agreed that, having seen the gliders, we preferred the L.C.A.s to which we were accustomed. The evenings were spent in the consumption of vast quantities of beer in the messes of the various Airborne units. There is a great deal to be said for learning to know people in the most agreeable circumstances.

On our return to Bexhill we all felt that time was running short. Instructions were issued about the disposal of kit, most of which we preferred to leave in our billets in Bexhill or Lewes, rather than send it home, where the sudden arrival of a mass of luggage would be bound to cause alarm. We felt, too, that it was safer to leave it all in a billet than in a base storage dump, open to the ravages of the vultures, who in C3 cloak thrive in every base. Our operational equipment we checked and rechecked, then rechecked again. One day we were all issued with will forms which were to be completed, irrespective as to whether we had anything to leave or not. We became honorary members of the British Legion, and we were urged to join the Old Comrades' Association. It was the third week of May.

Each day all riflemen, tommy-gunners and Colt men did half an hour's firing, mainly at tin cans on the beach and at pieces of floating wood. As always, I was amazed at the accuracy attained by some of the tommy-gunners, amongst whom old Donkin was about the best. I used to stand beside him on the beach, facing the sea, while he faced inland. Then I would throw three or four tins as far out to sea as possible in different directions, wait till they were floating well, then give him the signal to turn. He would bounce round on his slightly bandy legs, time his bursts so that the tins were on the crest of a wave as he fired, and with an almost frightening economy of fire he would sink the lot, straighten up and say: "That'll be another pint you owe me, sir. Ah canna go on givin' you young chaps lessons for nowt. Wy, w'en ah was a young soldier, we 'ad to learn the 'ard way!"

Inside the troop we checked on each section, subsection and group within the subsection. We appointed new N.C.O.s. Len sent for McVeigh, who had always steadfastly refused promotion.

"Look here, McVeigh, we want you to take a stripe. Now I know you've always refused before, but I should think it's fairly obvious that we're getting near something big now, and it's up to every many who's got it in him to do his damnedest. Whether you like it or not, you're a man who's got influence in the troop, so it's up to you to use that influence with, and not against, your N.C.O.s and, incidentally, your officers."

The little black eyes flickered in the square face. He was standing stiffly to attention. "May I speak to you, sir, kind of man to man like?"

Len nodded. The stiff figure relaxed.

"Well, look 'ere, sir, you know 'ow I feel about stripes—I've 'ad 'em afore, but they've never bin worth the trouble. Now we've got a good troop 'ere, ar! an' good N.C.O.s an' all, so if you want me to take a stripe I'll do it, sir, but just let me make one condition, sir—if we're not in action inside of six weeks, I can turn the things in again!"

Len grinned. "I don't normally make conditions, McVeigh," he said, "but this time I'll take you on that."

Tension grew as the days went on. The weather was perfect, training was over. All that we knew of our coming task was that we were to land somewhere, dash through a town, cross an anti-tank ditch to attack a battery, then go flat out inland to link with the Airborne, some of whom would have dropped in the night before the seaborne landing. We knew no place-names, we had seen no aerial photographs.

The task of writing normal letters home became increasingly hard. All mail was censored. In the evenings we drank.

One morning Len said casually: "Did you know that David Haig-Thomas has gone?" I stared at him. David was to be a sort of liaison officer between the Airborne and ourselves, and was going to drop with the first of the paratroops, prior to our landing.

"Gone?" I said stupidly. "Things must be getting sort of close!"

Len nodded. "That's right," he said. "It won't be long now."

Nor was it. On 23 May a move order was issued to the effect that the Commando would parade with operational kit the next morning at 05.30 hours at the station. When we entrained it became known that we were heading for Southampton, where we were taken in transport to a huge tented camp, where we settled down to await whatever was to come next.

The first day or two were spent pleasantly enough. There was a cinema tent with frequent shows. Loudspeakers blared out jazz most of the time. We lay around in the sun listening to Doc Patterson giving lectures on how to inject morphia into a wounded man, what to do when we ourselves were wounded, how to evacuate casualties, and general first-aid. He became increasingly cheerful as he warmed to his subject, and we felt worse and worse.

When we began briefing, however, we had plenty to keep our minds occupied. There was a model of the whole landing area, which had been made by Lance-corporal Brian Mullen, the artist, who unfortunately did not live to see the ground whose contours he had so faithfully and so painstakingly reproduced. The outline of the Brigade plan was fairly simple. We were to form the extreme left flank of the whole invasion. No. 4 Commando would land first, just after low tide (so that any beached craft would be floated off the beach), and would cross the beach, which at that time would be between two hundred and fifty and three hundred yards long, up to the dunes. We would then form up in an assembly area of demolished houses, before moving with all possible speed into the town, where we would dump our rucksacks and go into the assault of a battery situated at the mouth of a river and a canal, which could cover the landing beaches. The rest of the Brigade would in the meantime land and push straight inland to link with the paratroops and glider troops of the 6th Airborne, who would be holding two vital bridges.

After dealing with the battery we in No. 4 would tag along at the rear of the Brigade as far as the bridges. Once across them the whole brigade and the Airborne would seize and hold certain strategic points on the far side of the river to form a bridgehead. This bridgehead would be held at all costs until other troops went through, then the Brigade would be withdrawn and would probably do another landing elsewhere, though this latter part of the plan was of necessity somewhat vague, as it depended on early results and the number of casualties sustained. One thing was to be quite clear, the Brigade was at all costs and no matter what casualties to fight its way inland and link with the Airborne, and once across the river we were to hold on without giving ground, to maintain the bridgehead.

The next few days passed in a maze of photographs and models of the area. One reproduction was perfect right down to the last house, and had been made from the latest aerial photographs of the area. Every street, every pill-box, every gun and every wire obstacle was shown, along with possible searchlights and flamethrowers. There were photographs of the battery itself, which we studied with avid interest. We saw the gunpits, the anti-tank ditch, believed to be mined, and we saw a large white square in the middle of the battery itself. This was a large white tower, some sixty feet high, but we were assured that it would be white rubble when we got there.

The support for the landing was to be on an enormous

scale. The whole of the invasion and rear areas were to be bombed for days beforehand, in addition to the "normal" bomber raids. Then on the night of the crossing a force of Lancasters was to attend to the left-flank area while other forces dealt with the other areas. This bombing would move farther inland as the landing forces approached the shore and would then concentrate on the enemy supply and reinforcement routes. Fighter cover was to be on such a scale that there would be little or no interference by enemy aircraft. All our own aircraft were to have black-and-white stripes running across the underside of the wings for quick and easy recognition.

From the sea, warships like the *Ramillies* and *Warspite* would pound and batter the defences along the coast. This would continue until the landing craft were close inshore, when the barrage would lift and would remain on call to F.O.B.s, or Forward Officers Bombardier, who would land with the assault waves and who could, if necessary, direct the fire of the "battle tubs" on to any particularly troublesome stronghold.

In the intervals between the briefing we checked the kit yet again, went to the cinema tent and ran a sweepstake on when we would leave the camp and embark. Thousands of Yanks shot thousands of dice. Grimy cards were almost worn through. The padres were busy.

On the last day of May we were given the order: "Stand by to move." Dust rose in clouds as the Commando marched troop by troop to the embussing point by the main gate, where the T.C.V.s* stood waiting. They took us down to the docks, where the *Astrid* and the *Maid of Orleans* lay berthed. The weather was still fine. Lord Lovat came on board and wished us happy landings. He stressed the part we were about to play in history by taking a leading part in the biggest assault landing of all time. We put out to sea.

But the first few days of June, which we spent in Southampton Water, brought a deterioration in the weather. The skies were flecked with clouds, the wind

* Troop Carrying Vehicles.

freshened, white horses showed on a grey sea. A whisper of doubt ran round the ship. Peter and I stood leaning on the rail, looking at the huge armada of ships of all sorts and sizes which surrounded us.

"Surely they can't put it off now, it's gone too far," he muttered. I shook my head. I felt inevitably committed to an enterprise which might still be too big for all of us.

"They'll not call it off now," I said.

Len joined us. "It's on," he said.

We turned towards him. He glanced at his watch.

"Skipper's to make an announcement in about ten minutes," he said; "the bar's open, so we've just about got time for a drink first." He paused for a moment and gazed out across the water. The sun's last rays were giving way to midsummer gloaming, the world seemed to be holding its breath.

"With a bit of wangling," said Len, "I might have been in the N.F.S. in Newcastle."

Peter laughed and chanted: "It serves you right, you shouldn't have joined, it bloody well serves you right."

We moved towards the bar. . . .

CHAPTER III

. . . know ye not
Who would be free themselves must strike the blow?
BYRON: *Childe Harold*

REVEILLE on the morning of 6 June, 1944, was at
03.30 hours. In the Officers' Mess on board the *Astrid*
we were plied with bacon, eggs, toast and coffee—a magnifi-
cent meal. As I sat down at the table, I felt a strange tighten-
ing of the stomach muscles. The others I think were
suffering the same way, but we still managed to do justice to
the meal in spite of the tension.

There followed the bustle of getting into equipment,
easing the harness into as comfortable a position as possible,
slinging bandoliers of ammunition, stowing grenades,
magazines, field dressings and shell dressings.

Dawn was breaking grey over the sea. It was cold and
unpleasant. In the few minutes before "boat stations" most
of the men were looking eagerly about and chattering
amongst themselves excitedly. In the midst of all this there
was a loud explosion on the port quarter, and in a lurid
orange glow, one of the escorting destroyers broke in two.
We later learned that it had been struck by a torpedo. It was
the most depressing sight imaginable. The two halves of
the stricken ship reared up out of the water like an inverted
V and slowly, slowly sank into the leaden waves.

The order to take up boat stations came as a welcome
alternative to watching it, and in silence we fell in on our
craft. As each craft was filled, it swung outboard into a
twenty-foot swell, to pitch and toss a stone's throw from the
parent ship, while the others were lowered away.

On the run in, it was impossible not to be thrilled by the
happenings round about. Aircraft scurried to and fro in
the lightening sky above, all with a mission, all independent,

64

and all beautifully ours. Shells from the *Warspite* and *Ramillies* were screaming overhead, destroyers fired salvo after salvo, and soon we heard a new sound—the roaring swishing of the missiles from the rocket ships. The whole coastline was now under a thick pall of black heavy smoke.

In the L.C.A.s most of us were sick as dogs. In my own assault craft, I looked to where the shore loomed nearer. I could see the stakes and obstacles now. Two hundred yards to go. The barrage would be lifting now, but the noise seemed much the same. I looked round the boat. Thirty-two pairs of eyes seemed to be fixed upon me. Panic seized me. My mouth was dry. God don't let me do anything idiotic. Please let me seem normal. I glanced round at the faces I knew so well—Notman, ginger-haired, dour, sitting nursing the nozzle of his flamethrower; young Kavanagh, at eighteen the youngest member of the troop, a fresh-faced, clear-eyed boy from Dublin; the stocky, compact figure of the Sergeant-major. Confidence surged up in me. I looked across at our other craft, and saw Len and Peter give thumbs up through the spray. As I turned back, McVeigh who was in the Bren-gunner's place beside me, turned a green face towards me and said: "For Chrissake get me ashore!" I felt cheered. Someone was in worse shape than myself. Fifty yards to go. I looked at Trevor Hansell, R.N.V.R., who nodded and said: "Any time now." I shouted: "Prepare to land!" The obstacles loomed up all around. There seemed a lot of noise still. Dimly I realized it was no longer our barrage but their counter-fire trying to hit the craft as they came in. Thirty yards to go. . . . Twenty. . . . "Ramps down!" There was an almighty crash under the ramp and a spout of water as a mortar bomb exploded, the craft shuddered, the ramp stuck, I kicked at it and it dropped. . . .

Stumbling thigh deep in the water, top-heavy under the rucksack's load, I grabbed at one of the obstacles to steady myself. Dimly I remembered the warning about them. "Remember all of you, they'll probably be either mined or booby-trapped in some way or another." I hoped this one wasn't. The water on my left seemed an odd colour; it was swirling round a threshing red stump, which was all that was left of an arm, the body attached to it was invisible under the churning water. I splashed forward into the shallower water and up on to the smoke-laden beach. Through the wreaths of smoke I could see the hazy outline of the ridge of dunes. The air was full of peculiar whines and whizzing, while the clumping of the mortars and the tearing, searing rattle of machine-guns seemed to dominate everything.

Our L.C.A.s seemed to have beached fairly well, although it was difficult for me to see clearly through the drifting smoke. Over to the left the two French troops were having a hell of a job disembarking from their craft—two awkward L.C.I.s, which were badly-designed craft. Each of these vessels had two narrow ramps for'ard on deck, and when these were lowered from the high bows they invariably struck the beach as the boat came in, which forced them aslant, and made it impossible for the troops to run freely down them. This had happened to the French, and in addition, one ramp on each craft had been hit by mortar or shell fire. Eventually the maddened troops, who were crowding the decks, where they were being struck down within sight, almost within reach of their native soil, hurled scaling nets over the side and swarmed down into the water and thence to the beach.

As I splashed out of the water, I found one of the men from Peter's section lying just above the water-line. He saw me, and I could see that he was calling to me. I bent over him. He had been caught by a burst of machine-gun fire, which had slashed across his thighs, and his legs were almost severed. I tried to undo the harness of his rucksack, whose weight was holding him to the ground, but he had fixed it somehow to his belt and equipment. I had to leave him. My section stumbled out of the water past him, and we moved on up the beach. . . .

"Stop a minute, sir, for Christ's sake. . . ." Through a red mist of pain he heard the words and was vaguely sur-

66

prised to recognize the voice as his own. He knew old Mac couldn't stop, he'd thirty men from the other boat waiting in the water behind him, some weren't even off the L.C.A., how could he stop? The pain welled again and he moaned slightly and tried to ease himself into some less agonizing position. There seemed to be a crushing numbing weight across his thighs. Dimly he heard the answer to his plea: "They'll be down for you in a minute, lad," and saw the officer lurch past, bent under the weight of his rucksack, with the rest of the chaps splashing out of the water behind him.

As they passed, some shouted encouragement to him, though he couldn't hear the words above the chatter of machine gun fire and the ever increasing clumping of the mortars. The majority, however, were too intent on the job in hand to notice him lying there, just above the water line, a crumpled brown figure in a ghastly red pool.

The last of his troop had gone now and though other troops were landing only a few yards away a frightful loneliness descended upon him.

Frantically he tore at the shoulder straps of his imprisoning rucksack and in a frenzy of fear he fought to rid himself of the weight that held him pinned to the ground, but his efforts served only to jar and grate his shattered thighs, and a wave of nausea came over him. He lay on the pack that was his anchor and felt the sweat drip into his eyes. He saw the other troops of the Commando come in, saw the ramps of the L.C.A.s go down, saw the lines of men splash down into the water on to the beach. Around and about the boats he watched the fountains of spray thrown up by the bursting mortar bombs and the spurts of the machine gun bullets in the water.

An open beach and two hundred and fifty yards to cross to the first enemy positions. He'd known it would be sticky, but he hadn't imagined it would be quite like this . . . and daylight too. On the way in, the naval bombardment had been terrific, and the aircraft overhead had seemed the complete reverse of Dunkirk—as yet he'd scarcely seen a single enemy plane just as in those far off days he'd scarcely seen a British. He craned his neck and looked up. Overhead above and through the smoke he could still see them. All ours. He strained round to look up to the beach. The first people he saw were the infantry company who were supposed to clear the beach defences. They'd got about ten yards then had got down under the hail of fire that had met them. Just like the Skipper said, what you do in training, you'll do in action, and that's how it had been.

We'd lost a lot of chaps though. Rucksacks seemed to be everywhere. All along they'd said they'd rather go in without the things and look at them now. Dotted all over the beach. If a chap fell in the drink with one of those on, he'd never get out at all. The drink. . . . Sharply he turned his head. They'd landed just under half tide so that any beached L.C.A. would be floated off, but the tide would be coming in . . . what chance had he then, with the water rising higher and higher. He'd drown like a rat. Maybe some had already gone that way, some who'd been hit actually in the water. But surely the Navy would have got them off as soon as they'd been hit. He was just unlucky.

The water was lapping round his feet. Maybe he could drag himself up a bit. If he did, his legs might come off altogether, there wasn't much left, and he'd lost so much blood by now he mightn't have the strength. But God, he'd have to do something. Get over on his face, that'd be best. then the rucksack'd be balanced on his back. Maybe he could do it gradually and save his leg a bit.

Slowly he eased his body over and took the strain of the shoulder straps. Slowly he began to pull to his right. So far so good, another little bit and he'd be able to flop the last bit and then lie on his face to recover.

By now the roaring in his ears had increased so that he could no longer hear the waves. The machine-guns seemed to have died down too. The troop would probably be among them by now. They'd sort the bastards out.

Only the mortars kept up their hellish crump-wump, and the splinters tore great scars in the sand. If anything, they were worse than at the start. Probably firing from about a thousand yards inland, with all the ranges taped.

By now the water had reached his ankles. He'd better make an effort . . . all he needed was to straighten his arms and flop down on his chest. Take the strain. . . . The sweat dripped from his pallid face, his breath came in sobbing gasps and his teeth clamped into his lower lip, he never felt the blood come. After an eternity of time he realized his arms were almost straight, then right on top of him he heard the rushing screaming roar as of a train bursting forth from a tunnel upon a peaceful world . . . his ears clapped to the shattering crump, he felt a dull thump in the shoulder and sank down into a welcoming darkness.

He felt cold and tried to move but couldn't. He was barely conscious and his mind seemed somehow adrift from his body. Laboriously he struggled to lift a hand to his face to rub the sweat and sand from his eyes. His hand felt as heavy as lead. It was all wet too. His whole arm was. He craned and couldn't see his legs. His whole body was awash. Queer, he didn't feel any extra pain with the salt water in his wounds. Come to that, he didn't really feel any pain at all. Only a strange numbness all over. Perhaps he was dead already and yet he couldn't be, because he could still move his one hand. So he must still be alive. He was shaken and choked by a wild spasm of sobs. He didn't want to die. Why should he have to die. He was married. He had the kid too. What were they to do without him? The tears blinded him. He could no longer see the water which crept avidly over his body, propped against the rucksack, but he felt the coldness enveloping him and realizing what it must be, his sobs changed to screams, then his voice cracked, he choked on a sob, and relapsed into whimpering.

Then, as he whimpered, he realized how tired he was, the numbness of his body was simply the tiredness, the fatigue which came at the end of a march. The rucksack which had been his burden, his cross, his anchor, was now his pillow.

Gradually the tranquillity of completion, the satisfaction

of achievement descended upon him and as he gratefully gave himself over to it, he understood. . . .

Lurching up the beach from the pathetic figure, lying so helpless in the wide puddle of his own blood I caught sight of Len Coulson just ahead of me and decided to stick with him. The others were following on, though they could not have heard my shout of "This way 'F'." All around there was a hellish din, which numbed the senses. I found I was moving forward in a sort of daze. It was an effort to think clearly. I looked around to try and see Peter as we moved forward. Under the huge hump of the rucksack, every man looked alike, shuffling forward under its weight like boxers to the attack. The H.Q. craft were disgorging their cargo of men now, and it was now that little Brian Mullen, the unit artist, who from aerial photographs had made a scale model of the whole landing area, was hit as he splashed through the water and would have sunk below the weight of his rucksack, if Corporal Lansley had not dragged him up on to the beach. Here, as he lay helpless, he was hit again by mortar fire, and did not live to see the ground he had so faithfully modelled.

Twenty yards up the beach we reached a line of men without distinguishing rucksacks. They were the assault infantry whose task had been to clear the beach and its immediate defences. At the moment they were committing certain suicide by trying to dig in where they were. Over to my right I saw one of their officers get to his feet, wave his men forward, run two or three paces and crumple to the ground. No one else moved. As we drew level, I kicked at the feet of the nearest man: "Get up you idiot and keep going." The man made no move. He was dead. So was the one next to him, while a third lay writhing in the sand, clutching at a shoulder that had been shredded by machine-gun fire. They all looked young troops, and I thought that the man who had taught them to dig in on an open beach ought to be there with them.

We moved through, and the mortaring seemed to be

growing more intensive. Several times I felt the hot blast of the explosion a few yards to one side or the other, making my eardrums throb. Just behind me, a Bren gunner was suddenly hit in the legs by shrapnel and sank to the sand, calling to the Sergeant-major, who happened to be next to him: "Sarnt-major, Sarnt-major, take the Bren, I've been 'it." Taff Edwards looked round, paused, and in that moment was nicked in the wrist by a tiny particle of flying shrapnel. As is the case with surface wounds, the blood spurted out, so he clapped his hand over it and snarled: "Take the Bren? Take the Bren? Can't you *see* I've been hit? Get up man, and take the bloody thing yourself!" Whereupon the astonished Bren-gunner, shaken into obedience, staggered to his feet, and carried the Bren very effectively for another fortnight without complaint, before being evacuated to have his wounds given the attention they required.

I found that my mind was beginning to function more clearly, I was thinking along the lines of the drill we had practised on all the landing training. We'd be reaching the wire soon, and I hoped a lucky shell had blown a gap and there were no mines left. I always dreaded the idea of mines; they made such a mess, and what was left quite often lived.

I could see the wire now, with what looked to be a sort of mound behind it. Peering forward at it through the haze, I was half-stunned by a crashing explosion just on my left. The air was hot, while the tang of cordite caught at my nostrils. I looked round to see little Tich Cunningham, our troop medical orderly, picking himself up from the ground and staunching the flow of blood from his legs. Cunningham was the smallest man in the entire unit, and on the last occasion when the whole Commando had numbered off from the right, his diminutive figure, topped by a shock of red hair, had been the left of the line, while his voice had echoed over the square: "Number four 'undredan' thirty-five SAH!" Now as he struggled with a field dressing he looked at me and said: "Them bloody Germans! 'Ow the 'ell did they 'it me an' still miss *you*?" It had been one of

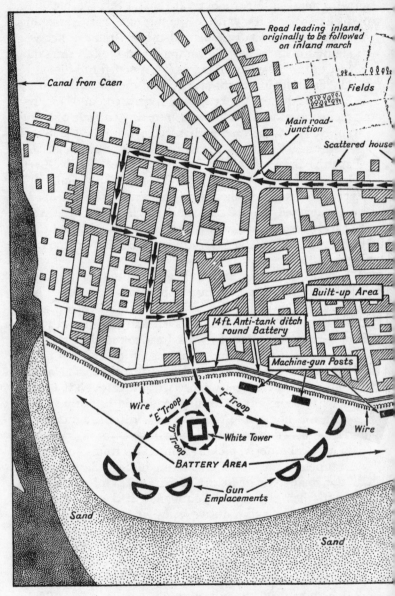

Canal from Caen

Road leading inland, originally to be followed on inland march

Fields

Main road-junction

Scattered house

Built-up Area

14 ft. Anti-tank ditch round Battery

Machine-gun Posts

Wire

"E" Troop

"F" Troop

"D" Troop

White Tower

Wire

BATTERY AREA

Gun Emplacements

Sand

Sand

D-day, 1944. Map showing the landing and attack on

72

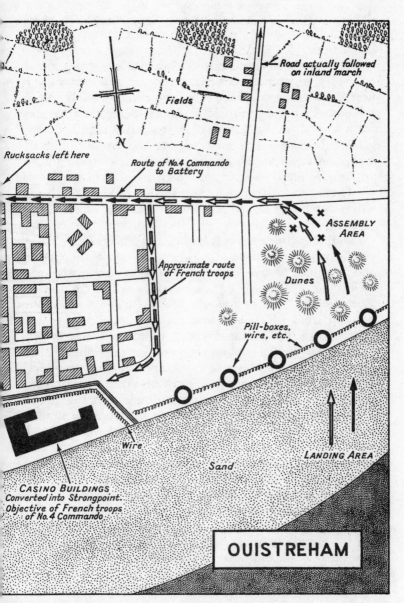

Ouistreham battery and Casino by No. 4 Commando

the troop jokes that as I'm six foot five, he would have to carry me back to the dressing station the minute we went into action.

The mound behind the wire was a pill-box, with a turret on the left which had been a machine-gun post. As we drew near the wire we could see there was still somebody in the pill-box. A tommy-gunner let go a burst as a figure appeared for a second at the entrance of the pill-box and a stick grenade hurtled out to burst amongst the wire. All of us in a position to do so, loosed off a round or two through the aperture of the bunker, if only to give vent to our feelings.

Then Len turned to me and said: "What the hell's Knyvet up to?" I looked past him and saw the slight figure of Knyvet Carr, dwarfed by his rucksack, scrambling through the wire. Knyvet was a regular officer of the Royal Artillery, who had been placed in command of the mortar and machine-gun troop, as this was the nearest approach to artillery we possessed. It was certainly not in his rôle as mortar officer that he was working his way round into a position from which he could throw a grenade over the mound of the pill-box at the machine-gun behind it which was firing in enfilade out on the troops on the right. A Bren gun fired burst after burst to give him cover as he scrambled up the slope of the mound. We saw him pull the pin from the grenade, pause, then lob it out of sight over the hump.

A moment later, after the burst, he stood up, but slipped under the weight of his rucksack, fell, and rolled to the foot of the slope, immediately below the pill-box. At the same time a stick grenade whirled out of the loophole and landed between the rolling figure and the wire. The burst of the stick grenade and the rattle of the avenging Bren sounded simultaneous, and none of us expected the slight figure to get up, but he did, unharmed but for a scratch on the wrist, and the troops began to swarm amongst the wire, past the pill-box and into the dunes beyond.

Two men inside the pill-box were still alive and active, but not for long; and a few others, who made a dash to some alternative position in the rear, were more or less riddled.

74

We saw the troops to our right dealing similarly with the pill-boxes confronting them as the whole Commando moved in an extended line through the beach defences.

These defences were typically German, both in structure and in siting. Each of the pill-boxes was a tremendously solid affair of concrete, with walls about 4 ft. thick and a roof of at least 6 ft. of solid concrete, surrounded by a thick layer of sand and grass. They were sited about fifty to a hundred yards apart, firing in enfilade with interlocking fields of fire. In most were a 75-mm. gun and light automatics. None of them faced directly to the front, but at an angle to either side, protected to the front by concrete and sand, yet able to fire very effectively in enfilade to either flank. Thus anybody approaching from directly in front could not be seen by the inhabitants, though he would be right in the field of fire of the neighbouring, covering pill-box. In support of each there were also individual machine-gun posts in emplacements with a revolving tank turret. Protection to the rear was not catered for to any great extent, usually being simply a machine-gun in an open position behind the pill-box itself.

Once clear of the wire and first line of emplacements, we looked for and quickly found the assembly area of partially demolished buildings. Here, a little off the beach, things were unnaturally quiet. After the chaotic din of the beach itself, which had been almost numbing in its intensity, it seemed extraordinary that we should be able to speak in a normal tone of voice here. Maybe the dunes were acting as a sort of baffle-wall, as we could still hear the constant thumping of the mortar-bombs, like a muted background behind us.

In the assembly area itself the whole scene was reminiscent of any of our landing exercises. Len and I found Peter, checking on the numbers of his section, and as mine came in I did the same. As I moved around among the encumbered troops, seeking out any stragglers from our own, I turned a corner of the building and bumped into a sergeant, whom I recognized as belonging to "E" troop. The tears were running down his face. He paused as he saw me, then said: "Mr. Wellesley-Colley's dead, sir. 'E just died, back there at the wire. 'E was 'it jus' as we come ashore, sir, but 'e picked 'isself up an' walked with us all the way acrost the beach. Then when we reached the wire, 'e couldn't go no further. I bent down over 'im, an' all 'e said was 'I'm sorry, sergeant, tell the chaps I'm sorry I couldn't make it' an' then 'e died, sir." He drew a slow breath. "I reckon we've lost a —— good officer." Then he moved on past me to join his section.

I returned to our own troop, where the Tommy-gunners were busy clearing their weapons of sand, and the remainder lay in their subsections waiting for the next phase to begin. The Bren-gunners were posted in various vantage points in the dunes, covering the landward side. It was still too early to realize the full significance of the fact that the beach had been successfully crossed, in spite of the failure of the assault infantry. Whatever came now, we were in a position to hit back, which on an open beach is practically impossible.

The next part of the operation was to be the approach through the little town on our left, culminating in the assault on the battery at the far end. The two French troops were to lead the way at the start, until they forked off to the left to make their attack on the Casino strong-point. When they left the main line of advance, "C" troop would lead the rest of us right through the town, till we reached the main road junction, where tramlines intersected. We would cross this, and at the third road on the left after it, we would turn down towards the sea again and enter the battery at the far end.

Following behind "C" troop through the town, "D" troop was to effect the entry into the battery, across the wide anti-tank ditch, while "A" troop, equipped with Vickers' "K" guns was to give the close support from the houses outside the battery. "E" troop was to take the gun-pits to the right, "F" the gun-pits to the left. Commando H.Q. was to take up a position about midway between the point where the French troops branched off to the Casino, and where we turned down to the battery, and would have "B" troop, with its mortars and machine-guns in reserve.

Within "F" troop, Peter would lead with his section, followed by Len with troop H.Q., followed by me with my section, until inside the battery, when the whole troop would make the attack on the three gun-pits.

The two French troops made the crossing in L.C.I.s, and had been on our left as we neared the beach. Their larger craft were hit again and again by mortar-fire as they closed inshore. Crouching below deck level, waiting the order to land, and watching the sailors of the crew lying tense beside the narrow ramp, which they were to run out as the craft beached, Guy Vourch struggled to maintain the calmness, the sang-froid he normally displayed to the world. His men had no such inhibitions. They were noisily discussing all that went on around them, and showed a certain keenness to crowd forward towards the narrow deck, craning their head from the hatch to try and view the approaching coast-line.

It was useless to order them back. For every one of them this was the return they had longed for, the journey home. It was also the long-awaited opportunity to drive the usurpers from their homeland.

Looking across, Guy could see the lines of L.C.A.s creaming their way steadily forward towards the black line of smoke which denoted the shore. He rather envied the British troops of the Commando at the moment. For them this was just an operation—a great operation it was true, but to a great extent an impersonal one.

He examined his own attitude to the coming landing. He found he was in a fever of tense expectancy. What would be the outcome of the invasion for him, for his family? Of his family he had little news. His third brother had had to leave France about a year or so before, and the last he had heard of his father was that he had been forced to make his way to North Africa, and that his mother and sisters had carried on the work of helping escaping pilots across and out of France. Whether they were still engaged in such work or whether they had been discovered, he did not know. He was looking forward to and yet dreading what he might learn on reaching home.

Not only did he fear for his immediate family, for his relatives up in Brittany, which at least had the advantage of being fairly remote, but in Paris, which for four years now had been defiled by the smugly mincing conquerors, was Brigitte. Tall, fair and lovely, she represented for Guy everything in life that was worth while. All through his long stay in England, when the majority of his ebullient compatriots had made the most of the moment and the opportunities provided, he had held himself aloof, directing all his energies to studying English, learning all that he could of the English way of life, for he was determined to return there after the war, to complete his medical studies.

This course he had pursued with the singleness of purpose that characterized all his actions. But now he was about to land in his own country. He felt the upsurge of emotion as he realized how much it still meant to him. The sailor beside him on the deck gripped the ramp. The crumping of the mortars was all around them now. The craft jarred, paused and lurched forward a little as she grounded on the gently sloping beach.

The sailor thrust the ramp out, it clattered along the roller and splashed into the water below, only to jut back some two or three feet above deck level as the way on the ship forced her further up the beach.

With yells of excitement, the French swarmed up on deck, Guy amongst them. The whistling of shells and the thudding of the mortars were implemented by the rattle of machine-gun fire. The ramps were shattered by a direct hit, either from a shell or mortar. Men threw themselves over the side into the shallow water around the craft.

"The nets," yelled a sailor. "Use the nets." He was pointing to the scaling nets which had been lowered over the side. They swarmed down into the churning water.

Guy, caught up in the fever of the moment, was yelling with the rest. He splashed from the water on to the firm sand of his native France. Away in front of him he could see the dark line of dunes, he lurched into a run, but had not gone more than a few steps when there came an ear-splitting explosion immediately behind him and he felt a numbing blow in his back and right arm. He was hurled forward on to his face, where he lay dazed, scrabbling weakly at the wet sand with his left hand, his mind still surging forward with his men as they hastened to close with the enemy holding the dunes.

As the numbness gave way to active pain, he made the bitter realization that the attack as far as he was concerned, was over for the time being, and the incessant crashing of mortar-bombs around him warned him of the need for haste or he might not even live to fight another day. He struggled clear of his rucksack and sat up. Round about him lay quite a group of his men, who had been caught at the same time as himself. Some were lying crumpled and silent in the churned-up sand, but others were, like Guy, able to fend for themselves a little, and were already trying to ease their less fortunate companions from their rucksack harness.

Behind them the L.C.I. was still waiting to float off. The crew, who had also suffered casualties on the way in, were wrestling with the shattered ramps, which had fouled up some of the deck tackle. As Guy watched, the wreckage fell with a splash into the water and the bows of the craft were free. Guy stumbled to his feet. He hailed the sailors on the deck of the L.C.I.; they waved back to him, and he heard a voice yelling above the din:

"Oright, chum we're comin'."

Guy could little more than let the words sink into his understanding. He was feeling sick and hazy, and every nerve seemed to vibrate to the explosions of the mortars. He stumbled to the other men in the vicinity, however, and shouted hoarsely to them to try and prepare themselves for the effort of scrambling back on board and of helping the more serious cases as they went.

A few moments later a naval party was on shore. Guy

had hazy impressions of strong arms half-lifting him through the water to the side of the ship. Then he was lifted on to the net he had so recently swarmed down, and was helped up on to the deck. With him were about ten of his men, some of whom were in a very bad way. As the ship floated offshore, Guy again gazed at the land. The beach, torn and churned still shook to the thuds of explosions but the lines of khaki figures—those who were still on their feet—had reached the dunes now and the machine-guns were silent. Filled with a sense of bitter frustration, Guy sank back on the deck of the L.C.I. as the shore receded.

The French troops, moving through the dunes, made their way down on to the main road running into the town. By now this road was being mortared from somewhere inland, and its hard cobbled surface made each exploding bomb the more deadly as it did not absorb any of the burst. The French, however, who had waited long enough for this chance, seemed to scorn any sort of cover as they swarmed along the road. Watching them from the dunes as we waited our turn to move off, they seemed to vie with one another to get there first.

Out in the lead, Phillippe Kieffer, tall, burly and determined, whose family was still in France, and whose son was at that moment fighting with the *Maquis* in the Haute-Savoie, pressed on towards the turning down to the Casino. His British signaller plodded along, panting behind him. As they neared the road junction a wild figure waving a huge French flag came bounding down upon them, yelling at the pitch of his voice: *"Vive La France!"* He embraced the delighted Phillippe Kieffer, then leapt upon the signaller, whom he kissed heartily on both cheeks. "Steady, Charlie!" said the signaller in disgust, but by now the stranger, who was a venerable old man with a white walrus moustache, was in an animated conversation with Phillippe Kieffer.

It turned out that the old man, whose name was Lefevre, had been the resistance leader of the district during the occupation and had been the source of invaluable information about the area. Now he was explaining to Kieffer, amid gales of laughter, how he had nipped out during the bombardment of the town area, while the German garrison had been below ground, and had cut the cables to the flamethrowers covering the beaches, battery and Casino, all of which were electrically controlled. Throughout the battle for the Casino this intrepid old man was here, there and everywhere in his efforts to be of further assistance.

Meanwhile the rest of us were pushing along the straight road that led into Ouistreham itself. "C" troop was well into the town by the time we in "F" were moving to the first crossroad from the assembly area in the dunes. This crossroad we reached as the last men of "E" troop were on it. Then came the screaming, rushing roar we had already learned to dislike as being too close for comfort. Flat against the sandy dune-grass, clinging to any dip in the ground, we heard the shattering crash of the burst, and were showered with earth, stones and bits of wood. A tangy smell assailed our nostrils as a cloud of smoke and dust drifted slowly into nothingness. Already Peter and his men were across the road. Automatically we scrambled up and hunched into a run. On the corner two still figures lay sprawled in the dust; both were dead. A third, the signaller, was kneeling with his head bowed in his hands in the shadow of the wall, making no attempt to move on. He seemed dazed, and as Len drew level he called to the man to keep going. The signaller rocked back against the wall, turning towards us a face that was just a splash of blood with a mess of congealed matter, which had been an eye. Wordlessly we left him.

We were now on the long, straight stretch that led direct to the centre of the town. On the right, or landward side, there was a single track line, which had probably connected Ouistreham with the next coastal town by tram. This had not been in use for some time, and probably would not be in use for some considerable time to come, as parts of it were simply masses of twisted metal. On our left, to the seaward side, we could now hear the almost continuous rattle of small-arms fire as the French went into action in their approach to the Casino.

My shoulders were aching as they hunched into the straps of the rucksack. We ought to be reaching the point soon where we were to dump the things. I peered ahead along the single line of lurching figures. No sign of the dumping area yet. There were more houses round about now, once attractive villas, with white walls and red roofs. Few windows were left now, and dusty cracked walls supported dilapidated roofs, whose broken tiles still slithered to the ground as we passed. In some of the gardens, trenches had been dug, either for protection or defence, but none of them was occupied.

The men in front were shedding their rucksacks now. Those belonging to the leading troops were stacked along the roadway, each with its 3-in. mortar bomb protruding from the pouch. That was mortar troop's only reserve of ammunition. Thankfully I eased my shoulders out of the harness and moved on, feeling curiously unsteady on my feet as I did so.

We were now approaching the centre of the town. From somewhere inland we came for the first time under shellfire. In my ignorance, I thought they were still mortars, but a gunner in my section, on hearing the first sharp cracking explosion after the quicker, more vicious whistle, said excitedly: "'Ey, thems guns!" to which McVeigh responded: "Wot d'you think they was, —— peashooters?"

Crouched beside a low wall, as the leading troops had halted, I looked along the line of men in front of me. One man suddenly stood upright, clasped his stomach and crashed forward on his face. The shot must have come from the windows of one of the houses opposite. The man in front of him turned and in that moment was shot through the head. He slumped and lay crumpled beside his friend. As I was searching the windows a Centaur tank clattered past us and opened fire with an earsplitting roar on to the gable windows of one of the houses. The window disappeared, and the enemy fire ceased.

We moved now by short dashes, with numerous awkward halts as "C" troop penetrated farther and farther towards the battery. Then we reached the main road junction. There were the tram crossings, and over on the right were a number of old disused street cars. One was leaning drunkenly against its neighbour. On one corner was a café in front of which a beaming figure in pyjamas was rushing from group to group, cheering and waving. *"C'est le jour!"* he was shouting. *"Le jour de la libération!"* My attention was caught however by what was happening at the other side of the street, where a young woman, sobbing distractedly, was being hurried indoors by another, older woman. I wondered what was the cause of their grief; was it simply a result of reaction at having had to contain and conceal their feelings for so long? Or had the girl perhaps formed some sort of attachment to one of the German garrison? After all, the Germans had not fought their way into that part of France, they had marched in with bands playing, while during their stay they had, from all accounts behaved with meticulous correctness. . . .

My thoughts were interrupted as the men in front of me got to their feet and dashed forward. I followed past the first side road, then there was a dusty track, and some twenty or thirty yards farther along, another road. For a moment I wondered about the track, and tried to remember the aerial photographs covering that part. Had the white lines of the roads all shown up the same width? I couldn't remember, I had been more interested in the battery. Anyhow, we passed another road, and on the next turning was an enormous bomb crater, through which we scrambled and dashed for the shelter of a wall on the right. We worked our way along it, then came another halt. I sat down and wiped the sweat from my brow. Len called back: "Check up whether the mortar men have still got all their bombs." The mortar men were close behind me. I checked with them and as I did so, I felt something soft and round under my hand. It was one single large wild strawberry. For a moment I thought of other strawberries, other summers. I popped it in my mouth. This whole thing was getting more like a training scheme every minute. Except for those odd khaki figures lying in a widening pool by the roadside. Funny how you couldn't recognize them as chaps you'd known. Just as well. We moved on down the road. On the right we could see the lighthouse. We seemed very near to it, and I realized we must have come too far along the main road. That track must have been a road after all. Another stop as we came level with some houses on the left. The sound of rifles and Brens ahead of us was much louder now, and more continuous. Some fifty yards ahead a tank was lying abandoned on its side. From the sound of the firing, I thought that "E" troop, immediately in front of us, must be running into trouble, and as though to bear this out, a grimy and bloodstained figure, grey of face, lurched unsteadily into view. It was a member of "E" troop. His wounds had already been dressed and he was making his way back to the beach. He passed us, unseeing, unhearing. We moved on.

On reaching the end of the row of houses, we found we had to bear left across an open space to a track, probably the one we had passed before, which now ran down the near side of the high white wall. The leading men broke into a double, and we followed on, slipping and stumbling in the loose sand.

Running with my section towards the track, I saw Peter and his men reach it, then turn right along the line of the wall. They crossed safely, and disappeared amongst some houses at the end of the track. Len and H.Q. began their dash to join the leading section. As my two leading men reached the track and turned, bursts of machine-gun fire from somewhere on our right flank slashed across the white of the wall a foot or so in front of them. They dived for cover, and as I dashed to where they lay, white dust arose from the wall as a flaky line whipped along it.

I swore and dropped flat beside the two leading men. We could not afford to have the troop split in two at this stage. The battery must be close at hand now and unless we moved quickly, the rest of the troop, who did not know of our predicament, would reach it on their own. We had about eighty yards of open ground to cross, all of which was covered by this damned machine-gun. I was not even sure which house the fire was coming from. I said to the two men beside me: "Try and see where they are," and shouted for the Bren. As the Bren gunner hurled himself down beside us, to be joined a second later in a whirl of white dust and sand by his Number Two, the two observers both yelled: "There 'e is!" and the nearest turned and pointed to a little window on the end of a house. "In there sir, I just saw the flash when 'e was firing at them two." I turned to the Bren gunner, a little Glaswegian, who already had his gun in position. "The corner house, the window at this end, the range'll be about two-fifty, keep firing in bursts while we all cross." He set his sights. "Right, sir." The Bren stuttered into action.

With the leading men, I scrambled to my feet and sprinted across the open ground. When we reached the cover at the other end the next group started, while the Bren sent burst after burst into the cavity that was the window. I was glad we had decided to use one in five tracer.

Once we had sufficient riflemen across, we could give cover to the Bren group as they came over. The difficulty was to stop them firing. They could not hear a shout over the noise of the gun. By good luck, they paused while the gunner fumbled for another magazine and heard me hailing them. While we kept up a fusillade on the window, the pair of them lumbered across. Once over, the whole operation had to be repeated to bring over the remaining sub-section. This time, the sub-section commander sent his Bren over first, then came little Cunningham the medical orderly, who by this time could barely limp along, much less run. The remaining riflemen and Tommy-gunners followed.

From start to finish, we could not have been delayed more than three or four minutes, and I hoped that the leading section had been held up for a minute or two somewhere farther on before they got as far as the battery. We set off at a run across the road into the rubble of a block of houses, where we found a man who had been dropped off by the other section to pick us up as we came along. As we ran, he showed us the route taken by the first party. We fairly tore along.

By now we were passing through amongst men of "C" troop, whose initial task had been to lead the way to the fringe of the battery. That meant the battery must be very close. There was still no sign of our leading section, who must have made good time.

I thought of the photographs of the area round the battery. I remembered very little of the surroundings except the wide anti-tank ditch which formed the outer perimeter of the battery itself. Immediately inside that had been wire, and a short distance inside the battery proper we had been shown the landmark to look for. This had appeared on the aerial photographs as a white square, which we were told was a solid building, some sixty feet high, built of white stone. It was primarily an observation tower, to control the fire of the guns in the battery. "But," they had said, "by the time you get there, after all the bombing and the shelling, there probably won't be any building. You'll recognize the white rubble though, and you'll be able to use that as a check."

I called out to a man as we passed: "How far now?"

"Just round that corner, sir, and you're right at the ditch," he answered cheerfully.

We swept round the corner, and my heart dropped to my boots. For there, beyond the ditch, tall, white and gleaming in the early morning sunlight, stood the tower, seemingly undamaged. Its completely blank face made it even more sinister. On our side there was no door, no window, just concrete. The only sign of life about it as we raced over the planks crossing the anti-tank ditch was the steady stream of stick-grenades that twitched and twirled over the parapet at the top....

After the first moment of abyssmal dismay at the sight of the great white tower looming up in front of us we had little time for thought. There to the left of the tower, some hundred yards from us, was the other section of the troop,

86

from which we had become separated during the approach to the battery. They were moving in extended order amongst the bomb-craters towards the gun emplacements at the far end of the battery enclosure. We ran out into the open after them.

Once clear of the shelter of the houses overlooking the edge of the battery, we came under small-arms fire which seemed to come from both sides, and buzzed and crackled around us in a most disconcerting way. The ground was churned and cratered everywhere, which made it difficult for us to make steady progress, although it probably helped to make us a more difficult target as we bobbed about amongst the huge holes. As we could not return the fire, there was nothing for it but to run, hope, take cover, then do it all again. We crossed about two hundred yards of open in this way, when the other section reached the first of the emplacements. Just then we reached two craters, beside which lay the bodies of two of the other section, and as we dived into the welcoming earth, a hail of bullets spattered into the ground around us. This fire could come only from the tower, which now lay directly behind us. Two-thirds of the way up it was a slit on the two seaward sides, normally used for observation but from which, in emergency, a machine-gun could be used.

I yelled to the Bren-gunner, who needed no second bidding. His gun clattered into action right away, and the odd tracers showed he was hitting in and around the slit. I looked at the two figures lying so still between the craters. Both were dead.

As we prepared to move off, another figure rose from a nearby crater and staggered towards us, dragging his Bren in his left hand. Petrified, we watched the stumbling man, who lurched towards us, then stopped almost at the edge of our crater and teetered, swaying drunkenly, on the brink. It was McDermott, strong, sandy-haired and argumentative, who had been hit in the right shoulder, and whose right side was now smothered in blood. White of face and with unseeing eyes, he swayed and as he did so a burst from somewhere feathered a line in the sand by his feet. Someone leapt up, grabbed him, and bundled him in beside the others. "Take ma Bren," he said, "an' gie us a rifle."

As they were relieving McDermott of his magazines, those who were watching to the front shouted out: "They're coming back!" And sure enough the thin line of men could be seen a hundred yards away leaving the emplacements and heading in our direction. I called to the Bren gunners to keep up the fire on the slit until the others arrived, but their firing was suddenly drowned by a whistling screaming roar followed almost instantly by a cracking explosion. Then another and another, until the whole universe seemed to be disintegrating. The ground all round us heaved and shuddered, earth and flame spurted with each successive crash, while the air was filled with dirty brown smoke and the tang of cordite.

Grimly, we hugged the loose sand, while the Brens still chattered at the tower. Then through the smoke came the other section. Dash, down, up. Dash, down. Len Coulson, the troop commander, hurled himself into the crater.

"Where the hell have you been? They've taken the big guns out, so there's nothing we can do over there. This shelling's getting worse, so we'll pull out to the road again. Follow us up when we go."

"Right."

Len crawled to the lip of the crater, dragged himself out and dashed towards the next, followed by Peter Mercer-Wilson and the other section.

In the crater, the Brens and riflemen still kept up a steady fire on the tower, and on a machine-gun post outside the battery which someone had somehow spotted amidst the hellish upheaval all round. We gave them a start of fifty yards, then group by group, we dashed after them, keeping well spaced out as we crossed the open.

On reaching the road, we found the other troops also withdrawing from the battery position, and "E" troop reported that their three gun emplacements were also empty of big guns. "D" troop in their first rush upon the

88

various defences of the battery area had taken over a hundred prisoners, while the crews of numerous machine-gun posts had been killed. At least it had been ascertained that the battery contained nothing that could in any way hinder the landings of the follow-up troops later in the day. For a short time we rested by the rucksacks, while there was some sort of conference. It was the first opportunity we had had to take a breather and though Brens kept up a vigilant watch, the men, lying in their sub-sections groups, smoked and talked of the happenings of the forenoon. I crawled into a hollow where Peter was already sitting.

"How's it going, Peter?"

"Oh, all right, I've lost just about half the section though."

"How many killed?"

"I think only two or three, but I'm not sure. I hadn't time to look, and one or two of the chaps who got wounded looked pretty bad. Still, they'll probably be evacuated quickly I should think."

"I expect so. Anyhow, we've not lost as many as I thought we would."

"No, but the other troops lost more on the beach than we did, I believe. What did you think of that bloody tower?"

The reply was lost in a sound that caused us both to shrink into the meagre cover of the hollow. A grinding rasping sound like a tramcar grating too fast round a corner. An unforgettable sound. We looked at each other as we clung to the earth.

"What the hell's that?"

"Damned if I know."

The answer came instantly as the whole field in front of us seemed to burst into flame.

"It's some sort of oil bomb or something."

"I hope to God they've only got one."

The nearest oily fire was about fifty yards from us and as we watched, we heard again the harsh warning. Again we waited and to our relief the burst showed up about two hundred yards farther away.

"It's about time we moved from here. There's no point in hanging around, is there?"

"Well, here's Len, so we probably will move."

"Good."

Len Coulson lumbered up. He had his rucksack on again and wasted no time in preliminary beating about the bush.

"On your feet 'F' troop, 'D' sub, 'C' sub, H.Q., and then the rest of 1 section."

The sub-sections filed towards the road. As they did so the Troop Leader explained the position to the sub-section leaders.

"We can't go up the way we originally meant to, as they're supposed to have some armour there still, so we've to make a bit of detour. It'll mean a slightly longer march, but we can still get there with bags of time to dig in. Whatever happens, we must get there. I can't do more than show you the approximate route, because some of it's across country and will depend on the lay of the land when we get there. But this is it as far as I can show you." He spread the map and we studied the unfamiliar names.

"O.K. Right, lead on 'D' sub."

We moved off, back the way we had come, almost to the assembly area. Then at the crossroads where the two members of "E" Troop lay, waxen and unrecognizable, the leaders swung left inland along a road which seemed to be devoid of cover. As if to bear out this theory, after they had gone only a short distance, shots began to crackle overhead and aroused in all of us an almost uncontrollable desire to bend double. But the old stagers laughed and recalled field firing exercises where the shots overhead had been a sight closer than that.

So we went on about a mile when, without warning, above the crackle of the machine-gun bullets, which still seemed to do no damage, mortar bombs began to burst in the fields on either side of us. Many were uncomfortably close, and we soon had to take advantage of what cover there was available. This might be a ditch, a house, a wall, a knocked-out Bren carrier or scout car, or simply a rut, depending entirely on where you happened to be in the column.

As the mortaring increased, I took a dive into the lee of a low wall and lay there. The men in front of me were already down. At the other side of the road I could see a Bren carrier, half on its side, its crew lying around it, except for one man who sat clasping his stomach and gazing stupidly at the thin trickle of dark red blood that coursed slowly between his fingers. He paid no heed to anything that went on around him and I wondered pityingly how long he would last, and what his thoughts were as his life trickled so inexorably through his fingers.

Suddenly there was a movement forward again and I brought my mind back to the business in hand. The man next to me jumped up and dashed twenty or thirty paces past the men of another unit, who lay along the edge of the road. I followed suit, and saw we had been lying behind a line of dead men. There were five in all and they had probably been either from the carrier or from a scout car which lay upside down in the ditch.

Then came a stretch of about fifty yards where there was no vestige of cover, no hedge, no wall, nothing. I looked behind me and assured myself that the two or three immediately behind me were up and running, and then made a dash across the open space. The sweat was dripping into my eyes, my rucksack straps were searing into my shoulders and with every pace forward, the weight on my back seemed to drag me back at least half a yard. I had neither the breath nor the strength to swear, but concentrated solely on the doubtful sanctuary of the hedge at the far side of the gap. The mortaring was increasing steadily and I imagined that the enemy must be fairly close, as the bombs were not as big as the last lot, they must be about two-inch. That meant Jerry must be on the hill on the left somewhere.

Thankfully I sank into the shadow of the hedge and waited till my breathing became easier. Only a few were across the gap. I checked up. The whole of the rear sub-section was across. That meant the troop was split again. The rest were probably behind those dead blokes we'd just passed and didn't realize they were dead. As long as the movement at the front wasn't too quick they'd catch up all right. I mopped my brow and prepared to move again, as there were signs that the chaps in front were getting under way. As I stuffed my handkerchief back into my pocket my eyes raised to the level of the opposite hedge and my heart leapt into my throat. I was looking into the muzzle of an unwavering rifle, behind which I could see the outline of a head and a pair of shoulders clad in some camouflaged material. For a moment I remained petrified waiting for what must be the inevitable end. Then I threw myself sideways and brought my own rifle to bear. The other had not moved. The muzzle still pointed as unwaveringly from the hedge at the same angle. There was no movement, no rustling of undergrowth.

Sergeant Jones who had instinctively flattened to earth beside me said urgently: "What's the matter, sir; what's up?"

"There's a man in that hedge, you can see his rifle, look, but I doubt he must be dead, or we'd have had it by now."

"The others are moving off, sir."

"Well, watch when you get up, just in case."

But there was no need. As we cautiously rose, there was still no movement of the rifle and on standing up we could see the red blotch on the otherwise waxen face. Somewhat sheepishly, I continued along the road.

We were now nearing a little village, where there were already some troops of an infantry unit. . . . We made our way forward and finally closed up on the leading troops who had turned off up a lane leading to the left, into a countryside of cornfields and hedges. The detour was now apparently over and we would bear left, back towards the original route to the bridges, where by now the rest of the brigade would have met up with the Airborne. We were told that there would be a halt of about fifteen minutes till

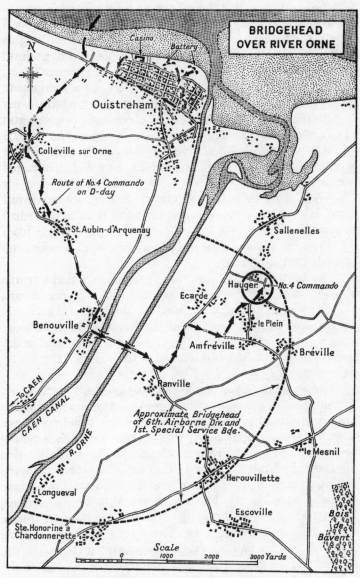

BRIDGEHEAD OVER RIVER ORNE

N

Casino

Battery

Ouistreham

Colleville sur Orne

Route of No.4 Commando
on D-day

St. Aubin-d'Arquenay

Sallenelles

Hauger

No.4 Commando

Ecarde

le Plein

Benouville

Amfréville

Bréville

To CAEN

CAEN CANAL

Ranville

R. ORNE

Approximate Bridgehead
of 6th. Airborne Div. and
1st. Special Service Bde.

le Mesnil

Herouvillette

Longueval

Escoville

Bois
de
Bavent

Ste. Honorine a
Chardonnerette

Scale

0   1000   2000   3000 Yards

D-day, 1944. Route of No. 4 Commando

the whole unit reached the village, so we squatted down in the street, backs to the wall and exchanged views on the curse of the rucksack.

"'Ow much furver we got to gow? This bleeding fing's gettin' me dahn."

"We should ha' left them on the *Astrid*, we could hae gotten them next week when we're picked up again."

"Battle order's what we should have had. You can get all you need into the small pack."

"Ah, but you wouldn't 'ave 'ad your candle and six foot of string. Nor your spare shirt. Nor your P.T. shoes or sweater."

"Well, who the hell's going to do P.T. now? An' if ah canny lay ma hauns on string or caunnles if ah need them, ah'm no' the man ah wis."

"Wonder if we've time to have a brew up?"

"Ah, that's an idea."

The brew up was, however, destined to remain as an idea, at least for a while. The remainder of the troop plodded wearily in and sank down beside them and another few minutes found the whole of the Commando there.

Then came the order: "Prepare to move," and once again shoulders ached and winced to the strain of the ruck-sack straps.

The way bore over to the left along a dusty cart track by a hedge. The line of men seemed insignificant as they wound towards the open space beyond the field. For most of us the whole thing had by this time reached the stage of being like the latter half of a scheme, the half where only the last slog home remained. The cart track was dry and the dust caught in the throat and nostrils. The hedge hummed with insects. The sun shone down on the drowsy Norman countryside. Looking to the left and back we could see the sea and landing area. There were craft of all sorts lying off shore, and little feathery trails moving to and fro showed the progress of the small landing craft.

We sweated, cursing, on our way. Field succeeded field and orchard succeeded orchard. The only signs of war were the odd bodies of German snipers sprawling by the hedge row.

As the track ran clear of the hedge and orchard on to a fairly open plain, we could hear tracked vehicles over to the right on what used to be the main road. The sound came nearer and a cloud of dust some half-mile away denoted the approach of the leading tank. It came clattering up towards us and was about two hundred yards away when there was a screaming stuttering roar from overhead and we had the first view of the Luftwaffe. Five bombs straddled the field between us and the tank, the plane swooped in low, machine-guns twinkling, overshot the tank, zoomed and was shot down by three avenging Spitfires which appeared from nowhere.

"Good show," said the troops approvingly and struggled on.

Beyond the plain, the track again ran between orchards and cornfields into a village. Here we stopped, and by wireless ascertained the position of the rest of the Brigade. As we sat on steps and on the kerb, ancient beady-eyed villagers tottered out and offered us cider. Only the very old were to be seen. Of the younger generation there were only occasional glimpses of sullen, lowering faces behind the white lace curtains. The spirit of France lived on apparently in the old; the young seemed to have sold their souls to the German invader.

"They don't seem hellish glad to see us, do they?"

"They probably don't know yet, how long we're going to stay."

"Well, they'd better start getting used to us then."

The column moved off again, this time down the side of the main road. There was the sound of firing some distance ahead. We passed an enemy mortar position, hastily vacated by all save one dead German. Piles of German equipment lay along the roadside, a helmet or metal respirator container, a belt or set of pouches, a shattered rifle. As the road bore right between sloping embankments surmounted by rustling corn, we glimpsed

95

the roofs of another village with a silvery streak beyond. That must be the river, and at the bridge we'd meet up with the Airborne. We came into the hollow and trudged up the other slope to the village. The sound of firing was by this time much louder.

In the village, the first thing we saw was a gloomy-looking bunch of prisoners clad mostly in their camouflaged suits, standing bareheaded against the wall. Sitting opposite them, one trouser leg ripped from the thigh to ankle and caked in blood with bloodstained bandages showing through the tear was a paratrooper. His helmet straps hung loose, a cigarette dangled in the corner of his mouth, his wounded leg lay across a second chair, and he cradled his sten. He grinned at us.

"You number 4? The rest of your crowd went through not so long ago. Didn't expect you for a bit yet. They're counter-attacking towards the bridges I think."

We went on.

Once through the village, the road sloped down to a left-hand bend, and as we rounded this bend a burst of shots spattered the trees on the right. We dropped swearing into the nettle beds by the side of the road and tried to see where the shots were coming from. This, however, was completely impossible owing to the amount of foliage round us. About fifty yards in front of us we could see figures in British uniform moving amongst the trees on the left of the road. The shots still cracked overhead, so we were apparently not the target. That was a comfort. We decided to move on up to the next corner, from which we might at least see what was going on. The leading sub-section struggled out of the nettles, and had no sooner done so when there was a red streak followed by a vicious ear-splitting crack overhead, and we dropped, with ears singing, back into the welcoming nettles.

"Jesus Christ, wot was that?"

"Dunno, but it weren't no three-owe-three."

"Sounded a bit near, didn't it?"

"Wot a bleeding bang too. They want to cut that out."

wird, das heisst: dass sie durch die deutschen
Truppen, wo immer sie auch auftreten, rücksichts
los im Kampf niedergemacht werden.

3.) Ich befehle daher:
Von jetzt ab sind alle bei sogenannten
Kommandounternehmungen in Europa oder in Afrika
von deutschen Truppen gestellte Gegner, auch
wenn es sich äusserlich um Soldaten in Uniform
oder Zerstörertrupps mit und ohne Waffen han-
delt, im Kampf oder auf der Flucht bis auf
den letzten Mann niederzumachen. Es ist
dabei ganz gleich, ob sie zu ihren Aktionen
durch Schiffe und Flugzeuge angelandet werden
oder mittels Fallschirmen abspringen. Selbst
wenn diese Subjekte bei ihrer Auffindung schein-
bar Anstalten machen sollten, sich gefangen zu
geben, ist ihnen grundsätzlich jeder Pardon
zu verweigern. Hierüber ist in jedem Einzel-
fall zur Bekanntgabe im Wehrmachtbericht eine
eingehende Meldung an das O.K.W. zu erstatten.

4.) Gelangen einzelne Angehörige derartiger Komman-
dos als Agenten, Saboteure usw. auf einem
anderen Weg, - z.B. durch die Polizei in den

Facsimile of part of Hitler's order to kill all Commandos: paragraph 3
reads: "I therefore command: From now on German troops will destroy
to the last man all enemy troops taking part in so-called Commando
operations in Europe or in Africa, whether it is apparently a case of
soldiers in uniform, or of sabotage troops, with or without weapons,
whether in battle or whilst escaping. It is immaterial whether they are
brought into action by sea, air or parachute. Even should these creatures
when discovered show their readiness to surrender, they are on no
account to be shown the slightest mercy. In each instance a detailed
report on this subject is to be rendered to the O.K.W. (German Supreme
Command) for publication in the Wehrmacht Report."

The officers of "F" troop: (*left to right*) the author, Len Coulson and Peter Mercer-Wilson.

Pat Porteous, V.C.

SOME OF
THOSE WHO FIGURE
IN THIS BOOK

(*Left to right*) Knyvet Carr, Guy Vourch and Robert Dawson.

Photograph taken by David Style during the Dieppe raid showing the gulley up which his troop ("C" troop) made its way from the beach.

Return from Dieppe: Lord Lovat (*left*), Bill Boucher-Myers (*right*) and Gordon Webb at Newhaven.

Return from Dieppe: Len Coulson (*right*) and Gordon Webb.

Patrick McVeigh, D.C.M.

Briefing for morning training in the Highlands at Braemar.

(*Right*) Snipers' course at Aberdovey. In the foreground, Guardsman Spearman; in the right background Lance-Corporal Harry Cunningham, troop medical orderly.

The Normandy landing: men of No. 4 Commando on the beach.

Men of the Commando making towards the Assembly Area.

No. 4 Commando in the Assembly Area after landing.

German strong-point on the beach at Ouistreham.

No. 4 Commando moving up to attack Ouistreham battery.

The tower of Ouistreham battery seen from the Casino. The Commando attacked from the direction of the buildings on the right.

M. Lefevre, French Resistance leader, who cut the power cables to the German flamethrowers in the beach defences.

The first rest: No. 4 Commando moving up to join the remainder of
No. 1 Special Service Brigade. In the centre (wearing beret) is Gordon
Webb, and, hatless, behind him is Len Coulson. The author is standing,
back to camera, on the right-hand side of the road.

Men of No. 1 Special Service Brigade H.Q. digging in near the Orne bridges. In the background are gliders of the 6th Airborne Division.

The remains of "F" troop at Bréville.

Len Coulson with "D-day" and "D-plus-one."

The landing area at Flushing. The tape was laid by the first troop of No. 4 Commando to land, and followed by the remaining troops.

The sea front at Flushing: the part shown adjoined the barracks cleared by the author's troop. On the front is the strongpoint covering the promenade and inland to the crossroads.

French troops of No. 4 Commando marching out of Flushing.

"I'm going to write to the papers about this."

There was another hissing red streak, another ear-splitting crack and one of the branches of the next tree crashed to earth.

"'E must've rolled up a bloody great cannon."

"Wonder wot 'e's trying to 'it?"

"Don't give a monkey's, as long it's not us."

Another crack.

"Why the 'ell don't someone stop 'im? Wot's the rest of the brigade doing? Don't Lord Lovat *know* we're 'ere?"

Again the leading sub-section dragged itself out from the nettles and lurched into a run for the next cover at the corner of the road.

Once they got there they found an Airborne sergeant who said: "Keep down the road here to the bridge and run like hell across, because there's a sniper in a pill-box who's got about twenty blokes already. You'll find an officer down there."

We continued down towards the bridge as indicated by the sergeant and met the officer about fifty yards short of the bridge. He grinned as he saw us.

"Hello, Mac; never thought you'd get this far. You'll need to duck going over the bridge though."

"It can't be as bad as that if you're still here. I suppose you've been sitting boozing all day waiting for us to get here?"

"That's right, smashing bit of stuff in the café over there, you ought to drop in some time."

"I will. What else is happening?"

"Well it was fairly rough early on. Then nothing very much, but the last report I have is that they're counter-attacking in about battalion strength towards the bridge."

"This bridge?"

"Yes."

"That's all coming from over there on the right isn't it?"

"Yes."

"Well, we'll nip across and bear left eh? What were those guns a minute or two ago?"

"S.P. guns 88-millimetre. Look, when you go over the bridge, get down to the left of the road, because it does come under fire a bit from the right."

"O.K."

"Righto then, Mac, see you later."

"Cheerio, boy."

We moved down to the crossroads immediately short of the bridge, and I passed on the information we had just been given.

"Remember, flat out over the bridge, then duck down into the field on the left of the road."

The leading sub-section rose and as one man dashed for the bridge, which was a steel affair with solid steel-plated sides.

Once they were safely across I followed with my H.Q., then the other sub-section. Over the bridge, we bore sharply left past an airborne anti-tank gun, with its dead crew silent around it, and down into the field. On the right, within fifty yards of the bridge which had been its objective, lay the nearest of three gliders allocated to that particular task. All three were within one hundred yards of the bridge, which was a testimony to the navigators' ability. Here, we were in comparatively good cover, because the road itself was raised above the fields on either side of it, and as long as we were close to the road embankment, we were safe from small-arms fire.

The edge of the field was a muddy, slippery ditch, and after about a hundred yards we came to a second mud hole running directly across our path.

The first man tried to jump it, failed because of the rucksack and sank to his thighs in the slimy mud. The man behind him hesitated and the troops following up con-certina'd on the leading man. The Troop Leader ploughed forward.

"Look, Mac, we'll have to get on faster than this, we should be catching up on the brigade by now."

"Well we'll have to have someone at each side of this damn thing, pulling and shoving the chaps over."

"All right, but hurry it up. I'll go with the chaps who are over and you can catch me up."

"Right."

The first few were across now and the Troop Leader scrambled over to join them. Peter came up.

"Give me a hand over and I'll pull them if you can push them."

"All right, that'll be the quickest way."

So, with one pushing and one pulling, we managed to get almost the whole troop across. There remained but a few, and looking round for a means of getting myself over, I saw a rock in the mud some little way away.

"I'll get over down there and then we can drag the others over."

I shoved the last man at Peter, turned, and I had just reached it when I heard a shot, and turned in time to see Peter spin round and fall. I leapt on to firm ground and raced to where he lay, my heart filled with dread. But as I bent and turned him over, I knew it was no use. He must have been dead before he fell. In straightening to pull the last man through, his head and shoulder must have shown sufficiently above the level of the road for the sniper in his pillbox to take a quick shot.

I wondered how I was going to tell his people. And Mrs. M., with whom we had been billeted in Lewes. She had been so sure it was going to be Peter. . . . The last of the troop was now some distance ahead and I had to leave him. I determined to come back as soon as possible and see he was properly buried. Then I hurried on to catch up with the others. I forced my aching muscles into a run and kept it up until I came to the second bridge, over the canal. Here again, we had to dash across, although by now most of us were flagging visibly. Across the bridge, I still went on forcing my way forward, until finally I could see the figure of Len Coulson in front of me.

By now, we were going along a leafy lane, quiet and pleasantly cool, and the desire to sink down and rest was almost overpowering. The men were staggering with fatigue and the rucksack load was now an almost unbearable burden. I lurched painfully up behind Len, who just then turned, saw me and said:

"All right, Mac? Everyone get across? We've not much farther to go."

"Peter's dead."

"How?"

"Sniper."

We both stumbled on without saying any more. The lane wound right-handed up a slope and here we were halted. We had caught up with the rest of the Brigade.

The road in which we halted was narrow and dusty, with a bank surmounted by a hedge on either side. On the left, the bank sloped sharply upwards to a promontory, while on the right it fell away into a dip, criss-crossed by hedges.

Gratefully, we sank down into the luxury of the dusty grass by the roadside, one Bren-gunner in each sub-section being left manning his gun. Aching shoulders were eased from the biting pack-straps and cramped limbs stretched to the comfort of the prone position. The drone of insects in the hedges was soothing to the ear, and the waves of tiredness ebbing and flowing over relaxed muscles brought on a pleasurable drowsiness. Down in the dip one sub-section began a surreptitious "brew up." Once again the whole thing took on the aspect of a successfully-completed scheme. Only the troop leaders dragged their weary bodies to an "O" group.

After a short rest we moved on, and Len explained what had happened. Things were going pretty well, although some of the paratroops had been dropped in the wrong place, and as yet there was no news of them. The enemy had been putting in increasingly heavy counter-attacks towards the bridges, particularly from the direction of Troarn and Caen, which seemed to be held in strength. This had necessitated a modification of plan on the part of the Airborne and Commando troops, who had now the intention of holding a tighter and more compact perimeter than had been originally intended. There was not much farther to go, and then everyone was to get dug in by dusk, as the enemy would almost certainly counter-attack in increasing strength as they found out exactly where the British troops were. Casualties in the other Commandos had, as in No. 4, not been as heavy as had been expected, although No. 3 had had a couple of craft very badly knocked about before they reached the shore, and the casualties in these craft had been pretty severe. There wasn't a great deal known about the larger issue, although everything seemed to have gone reasonably well. There would be more news by the evening.

As we trudged along the road, which by now had developed into a main highroad, things were rather unnaturally quiet, except for the whine of the occasional shell passing overhead towards the bridges. Only the silent figures in grey-green uniform lying in the dust by the side of the road bore testimony to the battle of the early morning. We then came into a village where the struggle had evidently been bitter and unyielding. German and Airborne dead lay side by side where they had fallen in desperate attack and counter-attack. Here around their shattered two-pounder lay a complete Airborne gun-crew, while on the other side of the road, in the ditch and out of it, were the attackers. Mortar craters pitted the soft surface of the road, and the trees and house-walls were pocked and scarred by the fragments of the bursts. Those of the Airborne who lived looked up from their slit-trenches, grinned, and settled themselves to sleep.

There came another halt, this time in the grounds of some large mansion-house, and from there the various Commandos were marched to their own individual areas, where they were to dig in, stay, fight and if necessary finish up, in the days to come. Within the unit, each troop was shown its particular position, told its tasks and who was on its right and left, and was then left to dig.

CHAPTER IV

J'y suis, j'y reste.

M. E. PATRICE MAURICE DE MACMAHON

LATER that evening as I hacked at the roots which obstructed every spade-thrust, my thoughts were very mixed. We had landed, we had reached the battery, we had linked with the elements of the 6th Airborne who had been dropped there during the previous night. With them we were now to form a perimeter around the bridges across the Orne and the canal, over which Montgomery was later to send his armour. Much had been achieved, much was still to be done. Our casualties had been lighter than we had expected, about seventy per cent of the unit was still fit to fight. But good friends had gone.

I went on with my digging till Len Coulson called me over to discuss the troop position. Things were quiet, menacingly quiet. Since our arrival in the late afternoon, there had been no sign of the enemy. We had posted sentries at all vantage points in the position, one of them being up a tree, already conveniently equipped with wooden rungs, which the Germans must have used as a look-out post, as it afforded from the top a wonderful view over the countryside as far as the beaches, where we had landed. For our more limited purposes, we had a man about fifteen or twenty feet up, supported by his toggle rope, keeping an eye on the fields and hedges round about us.

All round our position were fields of waving corn, with thick hedges beyond them, which in turn were backed by woods. On our right was "E" troop, with No. 3 Commando beyond them, while on the left we had "C" troop, with "D" beyond that.

Len pointed out these positions to me from where we stood, then said: "At least the job's straightforward from now. That road behind us leads down to the bridges, we can't move back an inch from here. It's the same with the others, our whole perimeter is as small as we dare have it. So here we stay."

"D'you think they know we're here?"

"I don't think they can, or they'd have done something about it by now. It's a good thing, too, because it gives us time to get properly dug in before they do come, then we can give them a lacing as they come in. We must try and get headcover on the trenches as soon as possible."

"With all this corn here anyone could slink up to within a few yards at night and bung in a few stick grenades before we even knew he was there."

"Yes, we'll have to try and get some trip flares or something rigged up. But I shouldn't think they'd do anything like that the first night, because I hope they don't know exactly where we are."

The digging continued. With weapons lying within reach, as one man dug the other brewed up for the two of them. Our last solid meal had been about four in the morning. So we ate and dug, and the day drew to a close. We had fixed a system of sentry duties, whereby one man of each pair would be awake, but dusk brought with it an added wakefulness. An eerie silence crept from the woods which, at the other side of the cornfields, grew more sullen and lowering as the shadows lengthened. A sense of unease, of being watched by unseen eyes, of being heard by unseen ears came over us all. Some stimulant was needed, and just at the right time, it came.

Softly at first came the sound of murmuring engines on the evening breeze, gradually becoming louder and louder, till the planes came in sight. "They're ours," someone sighed in relief. Great heavy planes, each with a glider in tow. Wave upon wave, looming up, silhouetted against the fading light of day they came, and with their coming, the sense of loneliness was dispelled. Reinforcements. The rest, or some of it, of the 6th Airborne. The gliders cast off, circled then swooped silently out of sight behind the trees. With a new surge of cheerfulness we turned back to await the coming of night.

Before darkness actually fell, Len sent an order round the troop. "From this position there is to be as little shooting as possible. They can't put any attack on us in strength until they've got themselves organized and till they know exactly where our positions are. We're here to stay, so if we can keep quiet till we're properly dug in and ready, we'll be able to sort them out then. If anybody does come through our lines tonight, they'll possibly be paratroops who've dropped too far from the river, and who are making their way to our lines. So grab anyone, but don't shoot, unless you've no choice."

So we waited through the night. Hour succeeded hour. The rustle of the corn sent chills rippling up and down my spine. From a nearby pond, the harsh croaking of frogs at first seemed frightening in its nearness. This initial fright gave way after a time to a sort of fell-feeling of wakefulness, a camaraderie of the clandestine, forming a background to the thoughts running through my head. Then suddenly, I realized the croaking had ceased, and the sense of security gave way to something approaching panic. I peered out into the darkness. Why had the damn things stopped? All sorts of unpleasant reasons at once suggested themselves. As if in derision, the croaking began again, and I could feel the others relax as I did.

Then, however, stealthy footsteps resounded like the roll of doom in our by now over-sensitive ears. They were coming down the track behind us. Knowing we could see and not be seen, we waited, tense. The footsteps paused, and as they did so, there was a slight scrabbling sound, vague forms leapt out into the path, there came a scuffle and thump, and the thing was over.

Three miserable and obviously terrified Germans, carrying no weapons, stood in the none too gentle grasp of some triumphant members of my section. It turned out that the Germans were part of the crew of the lighthouse at Ouistreham. During the events of the morning they had made their way inland, where they had lain up till night, when they had set out towards their own lines, which they knew must be in the general direction of Sallenelles, a village a little way beyond our lines. We sent a man off with them to H.Q. and returned to our vigil.

During D-plus-one the enemy began to probe around. A bullet suddenly smacked into the tree beside the look-out, who could find nothing to fire back at. From then on, a constant sniping was kept up from the hedges at the other side of the cornfields, and never was there a trace to be seen of the firer. The same thing was happening all round the perimeter, and "E" troop in particular was harassed by fairly heavy fire, to which they replied with interest. Opposite their position the hedge ran in towards them till it was only about thirty yards away. In the evening we watched the last of the fighter sorties sweeping homeward as we prepared for the last brew of the day. As yet none of us had had more than about an hour's sleep.

The sunset was stormy, and a last look at the beaches showed no abating in the surf. Just as the sun disappeared from view and the red-flecked clouds were darkening, there came the roar of low-flying aircraft, and a lone German swooshed across the tree-tops and tore over towards the bridges, machine-gunning everything in sight. A few minutes later he returned, disappeared over his own territory, and darkness fell.

After half an hour of the exaggerated hush that follows the close of day, we heard planes overhead, and as the droning passed over, the first of the Ack-Ack curved slowly up to meet it. Within a matter of seconds it seemed as though every gun which had been brought across had come into action. The whole sky was criss-crossed by red streaks and hung by graceful constellations of glowing red spheres, which burst into gently-floating satellite spheres. Above the barking of the guns, we could hear the whine of the falling bombs and the rumble of their explosion far below. It seemed impossible that any aircraft could fly through that interlocking pattern of fire and live, and as though to prove this theory there was a sudden orange flash in the velvety sky and a sheet of flame began its downwards course of disintegration. A moment later, another followed it, then the aircraft droned away, leaving the lurid glow of fires to mark where they had been.

A short time after, dive-bombers swept the whole area, filling the night with shrill horror, but they did not stay for long, though they swooped low overhead and machine-gunned the whole area as they returned to their own lines. "Vicious bastards," said McVeigh, after he had ducked as they passed. "I'd like to 'ave one, one of these days, jus' for old times' sake."

As the planes departed, the enemy artillery opened up from a great range and began solemnly to fire one enormous shell every few minutes towards the bridges. First came the flash, a few seconds later the boom of the gun, then the whine of the missile as it passed in its majestic flight overhead, and finally, eleven seconds from the start of the whole proceedings, the rumbling crash of the explosion.

Throughout the night the woods on the German front were constantly illuminated by white or red Very lights, sometimes in the distance and sometimes quite near enough for any watcher to imagine that an approach march was being made, prior to an attack. But no attack came. Instead, there came a constant stream of paratroopers from the direction of the enemy lines. They had all been dropped in the area of the Dives instead of the Orne and had either fought their way through to our lines, or had lain up until they were certain of their direction, and then in the darkness made their way across. They were all sent on to H.Q.

The night wore on, until there remained less than an hour till first light. It seemed that another long watch had been unnecessary, when from the woods which housed "A" troop and the enemy, burst upon burst of machine-gun fire, punctuated by the thumps of exploding grenades, broke loose and tracers ricochetted out at all angles. The rest of the Commando sat tight and wondered how "A" were getting on.

In the woods, coming under fire from three sides, with no field of fire in which to give scope to his "K" guns, and no targets anyway, Alastair Thorburn very rightly decided to pull out into the main Commando position. So a signal was sent to H.Q. telling of their intention and, warning "F" to look out for them coming in through "F's" lines, sub-section by sub-section they withdrew, bringing their guns and their wounded with them.

When the warning was received by "F," Len Coulson passed the word round, and ordered the medical orderlies to stand by in case they were needed. We had not long to wait, for as the grey mists were beginning to lift with the rising sun, a line of figures loomed up along the track, and "A" came through. As they arrived "B" troop's 3-in. mortars came into action on to the position they had left, and plastered the whole area. This apparently had some success, for no further attack materialized and no fire was brought down in reply.

The next day brought an increase in the amount of sniping, which served to keep us all in constant expectation of the inevitable attack. Sleep, though we were all in much need of it, was out of the question. As the day wore on too, there was an almost constant skirmishing in "E" troop's area, where the cornfield narrowed.

The attack that was bound to come in strength sooner or later was constantly in our minds. That it would be on a large scale was certain, and as we knew there was no question of withdrawing or yielding any ground, we felt that the longer it was delayed, the worse it would be. But night came without any major attack having developed and, as usual, the day's wait was rewarded by the sight of the gliders being towed into the landing zone. Throughout the night, the bridges were bombed, and the area immediately behind us was mortared, while the woods in front of us were constantly illuminated by Very lights.

The morning of D-plus-three found us all red-eyed but still perky. The strange thing was, that as all the signs pointed to the attack coming nearer, the more cheerful did the troops become. In actual fact, there was little cause for cheerfulness. Supporting arms on our side were still desperately short. The storms at sea had prevented, or at least slowed down, the landing of guns and tanks, and there was not a single tracked vehicle across the Orne that was not German. From Caen came reports of enemy armour in strength, armour which could easily be deployed into the area of the two bridges held by the Airborne and Commando troops. Against armour there was at the disposal of each troop one PIAT mortar, with five bombs.

The lack of sleep was now telling. Thinking was a slow and laborious process. Men would sit, completely oblivious to everything that went on around them until some threat of action, when they would suddenly become wide-awake and energetic, only to relapse when it was over. In the early evening there came a situation report of enemy attacking in company strength on other units in the perimeter, and it seemed they were massing their available forces for a major drive towards the bridges.

Night came, bringing with it a sharp attack on "C" troop, the darkness and the growing corn allowing suicidal enemy to lie low even when their main force had been beaten off, then to open up on their own, with disconcerting effect. "C" troop suffered a number of casualties clearing their ground of these interlopers.

In the middle of the night the spasmodic shots and thumps of mortars gave way to a crescendo of fire coming from the direction of the strongpoint on the Sallenelles road. Machine-guns rattled, grenades thumped, and rifles fired in fusillades. This went on for some time, then died away quite suddenly, leaving us to wonder what it had all been about. I was lying discussing it with the sentry on the track junction, when we heard the sound of running feet and panting breathing. Together we waited, listening. As the figures drew near, one stumbled, and we heard an unmistakably English oath.

I got up in front of them and said: "Who the hell are you?"

They stopped and peered at me in the darkness. A flare gave a moment of light.

"Marines!" I said. "Where the hell have you come from?"

One of the group took it upon himself to speak. "Jerry's through," he said. "They're on the road."

I grabbed the man by the arm and rushed him up to where Len Coulson was with the main body of the troop, and poured out the story to him.

"Why the hell didn't they send out a signal?" he asked. From what we could gather, the enemy had launched the sudden attack on the strongpoint in some strength, using mostly automatic weapons, and after a sharp encounter had overrun the position.

This was more than serious as the position dominated the route to Sallenelles and to the bridges. It simply had to be re-taken. We got the news through to H.Q. as fast as we could. The nearest of our troops was "D" troop, so Pat Porteous was given the task. Pat, a stockily-built Regular from the Royal Artillery, had won a good V.C. at Dieppe. He earned another now. Within a matter of minutes after he heard the news, he and his whole troop, which had already suffered considerable casualties on the first day, rose from their trenches and stormed through the darkness in a flat-out assault, yelling like banshees as they came to grips with the enemy patrol, which outnumbered them by more than two to one.

Again, in "F" troop lines we listened to the sound of battle on our left. This time we listened tensely, trying to make out which way the fight was going. As the sounds died away a wireless message reached H.Q., reporting that the position was again in our hands. The encounter left "D" troop with two officers, a sergeant-major and twelve men.

CHAPTER V

They shall not pass. . . .
FRENCH TROOPS AT VERDUN

A<small>T</small> the end of the dawn stand-to on the morning of
Saturday, 10 June, we were all almost at the end of our
tether for want of sleep. I walked round my section again and
again simply because I dared not sit down. A man would
lean back in his trench as I spoke to him and would become
unconscious before my eyes. One man, standing in his slit-
trench, fell asleep on his feet, slithered slowly down to his
knees, to finish huddled in the corner, still holding the mess-
tin from which he had been eating when sleep overcame
him. Others slept the sleep of utter exhaustion in the
strangest attitudes, leaning straight-backed against a tree,
kneeling with head bowed on the lip of a slit-trench, lying
face down on the ground, still clutching their rifles.

Len's voice came slowly to me as though from miles
away. "Mac, we've got to keep awake. I think it's bound to
come today."

Nothing, however, happened till about nine-thirty,
when we were mortared for about half-an-hour. Then the
sun struggled through the clouds, and in the brightness of
the morning we were astounded to see two German soldiers,
one of them carrying a pack wireless set, strolling blithely
along the track towards our position. They were obviously
to report on the effects of the mortaring, and were destroyed
by about half the delighted troop from about twenty yards
range.

Thereafter we were mortared for five hours. The noise
in the orchards and the wooded park was terrific. The wood
resounded to the crashing of the explosions and the rending
of timber, while the descending shrapnel splinters kept up
a continuous rattle on the wall. This mortaring reached its

peak in the middle of the afternoon, the woods reverberated, and casualties in "E" troop, who had made the mistake of digging only shallow trenches under the trees, mounted rapidly.

Then came the visit of the Brigade Major. He arrived in "F" troop's position, and after grubbing about in various holes finally found the Troop Leader, who, like everyone else except the look-out was well below ground. The Brigade Major was immaculate in green beret and creased trousers and said:

"Have the men had a hot meal yet?"

"*A hot meal?* While this is going on?"

"Yes, certainly, they should have had one by now."

The Troop Leader leaned from his trench.

"Sarnt-major."

"Sir."

"Have the men had a hot meal yet?"

"A hot meal? Christ, no. Nossir."

The Brigade Major looked disapproving.

"Well, see they get a good hot meal right away," he said, and moved off. He went about twenty yards, there was an almighty explosion, a cry for stretcher-bearers, and back he came feet first, whereupon the irrepressible sergeant-major popped his head from his trench and called out:

"It's all right, sir, we'll go without, we're not really 'ungry."

At about five o'clock we saw the enemy massing directly opposite us at the edge of the wood, and at the same time, the F.O.B. arrived. An F.O.B. is a man who imagines he can control and direct the fire of a warship, which is generally some miles offshore. In this case it was the *Ramillies.* Len was more than doubtful. "These things fire pretty big shells, don't they?" he asked.

"Fifteen inch, nothing but the best!" said the F.O.B. "All I have to do is get on the blower, give the order, and when I say 'Shot One' you watch the edge of that wood!"

"All right." said Len, weakening. The F.O.B., delighted, manipulated his set, gave a few mysterious references, then

111

yelled "Shot One!" We all turned and fixed our gaze on the edge of the wood. For a moment nothing happened. We waited expectantly. Then, with no warning whatsoever, there was a colossal explosion, the ground in the middle of our position heaved upwards, and showers of mud and huge pieces of tree splattered down upon us. We clung to the earth while things subsided. Len turned a baleful eye on the F.O.B., who gulped and said: "I'm terribly sorry . . . but the next one'll be over there!" The reply cannot be recorded.

This episode was entirely responsible for the chilly reception which was given to the Airborne F.O.O. who arrived on the scene, almost as soon as the F.O.B. had crept discomfited away. The task of an F.O.O. is in principle the same as that of an F.O.B., except that he "controls" the fire of an artillery unit somewhere immediately in rear of the troops to be supported. This chap had some 25-pounders to fire, and laughed immoderately when told of the black his predecessor had just chalked up. However, as he was from the Airborne and seemed a pretty competent sort of chap, he was given a chance.

His system was quite different from that of the last one, and as he clambered up on to the wall, he cheerfully took stock of the situation.

"There's quite a lot of the bastards there, aren't there? Not much point just giving them one or two. Might as well shove about twelve rounds in right away, don't you think? How far is that from here? About two hundred yards? Mmmm. Well, we'll have a bash."

While the nearest members of the troop cautiously edged towards their slit-trenches, he gave a couple of rapid orders into his set, and before anyone knew what was going on, there was a horrible whistling overhead, and the edge of the wood opposite was hidden by a series of clouds of black smoke. The F.O.O. whooped in triumph, and the troop look-out, hung to the rungs of the O.P. by his toggle-rope, said with satisfaction:

"Just the job. Send some more."

Another twelve rounds were forthcoming, and the attack did not materialize. The F.O.O. climbed down from his wall. "It's no use asking for more," he said. "We're rationed down to twenty-four rounds a day till they get more ammo ashore and so that's the lot for today. So-long!"

And he went away.

This breaking-up of the attack seemed to infuriate the Germans, for the mortaring was stepped up to a crescendo of hate. The woods reverberated, and casualties, especially in "E" troop, were heavy. Hutch Burt, Troop Leader of "E" troop, was wounded, and as both his subalterns and his sergeant-major had been casualties on the first day, this left the troop without an officer. The senior sergeant was the next to go, and the troop was eventually run by a section sergeant. The troop strength was about a third of the original strength.

Then the German machine-guns opened up to give cover to the advance of their troops across the open field. When they were clear of the wood, our battle began. Of how long it lasted, I have no idea. I remember Len telling me to take the two mortarmen and tickle up the Germans as they came out. I remember lying in the orchard directing their fire, and listening to the enemy fire hissing through the hedge and sighing over our heads. I remember McVeigh, cuddling the butt of his Bren and yelling at the top of his voice: "Come out, ye square-headed bastards. . . ." while loosing off burst after burst. I remember Len Coulson, confident and alert now. I remember the German attack melting away, re-forming, then melting away once more. I heard Len say: "We've done it, boy, they're gone for good . . . what's left of them. I'll just get Knyvet Carr to shake them up with his mortars as they go."

The din of battle died away, and I turned to my slit-trench. It had been blown in. I dragged out my rucksack—it was badly holed and wet with the remains of the whisky from my flask, while the splinters from my camera stuck out from the shreds of my shirt.

I remember very little else, for while I was on my hands

113

and knees in the wreckage of my trench, I fell asleep.

This battle on D-plus-four ended the first phase of our sojourn on the Continent. It was a triumph for the whole unit, but we in "F" troop felt that it was also a personal triumph for Len Coulson. Prior to that battle, not one of our troop automatic weapons had been fired. The enemy probing around had not drawn any fire other than a few rifle shots. This may or may not have led them to believe that our machine-guns were there, but in any event, they had chosen our "killing-ground" to advance over in their attack.

To Len's foresight too, we owed the fact that our own casualties throughout the four days of mortaring, which culminated in the attack, were so light. Every trench had been dug deep, and as many as possible had then been covered over with some sort of headcover, which could keep out splinters. We had not yet reached the day when we were to fell trees and lay logs across the top, but nevertheless we did have protection of some kind.

The unit as a whole, however, had suffered fairly heavily. Of the 435 British officers and men who had landed on D-day there were now 160 left, while but 70 remained of the 200-odd French troops.

Almost as soon as the action was over news from the other troops began to filter in, and we heard how David Style of "C" troop had been wounded. In the midst of the battle, a white flag had suddenly appeared opposite "C" troop's position, and a party of about a dozen men ran forward. Mindful of the warning about the possibility of Poles wanting to desert from the other side, David had ordered the troop to hold their fire. The flag party approached. When they were some fifteen paces off, David stood up with a man on either side of him and called to them to come into the position. At once they dropped flat, and the hindmost man threw a stick-grenade, then loosed off with his Schmeisser. The stick grenade burst beside David's leg, shredded the calf, and killed the man by his side. As he fell, David was caught in the chest and shoulder by the burst from the machine-pistol which killed the man on the other side.

Our existence from now was different. No longer were we sniped from morning till night, no longer were we harassed by small sharp attacks. We seldom saw any aggressive enemy except at night, when single men, carrying wireless sets or packages of explosive often attempted to worm their way through our lines as far as the bridges or some place where they could lie up and direct fire by wireless on to places where it would do most good. By now too, we had a system of trip flares around each troop area, which to start with were regularly set off by stray horses.

At night, Len and I took turns in staying awake, half the night each. On one such night, I sat, cold and sleepy, huddled in a blanket behind the wakeful silhouette of the sentry. The time was just after four. Another hour till first light. If anything were going to happen, it would have to hurry up, or it would be daylight. I felt I was fighting a losing battle against sleep. Good job Carlin was there. My head drooped, my eyelids weighed like lead, then the whole world was lit by a dazzling brightness. Wide awake, I jerked upright, and in the brilliance of the flare stood a solitary German, rooted to the ground about fifteen paces away, blinded by the light and dazed by the suddenness of it. The tableau lasted one petrified second, then the German's ducking movement to the side and the sweep of Carlin's arm hurling the grenade were simultaneous. The flare died out as we ducked to the explosion of the grenade, and in the Stygian darkness that followed, we were unable to determine whether or not we had got him. Then from a trench on our right a rifle cracked. Almost immediately there was what seemed to be a colossal bang then an abysmal silence.

"What the hell," I said, "was that bang?"

"I dunno, sir," said Carlin gloomily, "but that grenade should've got him. He'd no business to get as far as thon."

"Well, we'll have a look in the morning."

At first light I went out with McVeigh, who was now the sentry, and dropped into the sunken track running away from our position. Soon we found him, sprawled at the top of the bank, struck down just as he probably thought he was getting away with it. Drawing near, we were surprised to see he had no head. Nor was there any sign of one lying about. We looked closer and saw that, from the clenched left hand still dangled the cord of a stick grenade.

When Carlin's grenade had gone off, and the live German had found himself, unscathed, standing as it were on the brink of safety, he must have decided to strike a final blow for the Führer. Tucked in the open neck of his tunic, he had a couple of stick-grenades, so as he crouched, he pulled one out, ripped the cord from the base with his left hand, and in that second, when the heads of the two grenades were almost touching, he had been shot; whereupon the grenade in his right hand had gone off, and had set off the other one. The resultant explosion had deprived him of his head.

"Wonder what 'e looked like," said McVeigh, curiously.

"Let's find his paybook and look," I said. A quick search of the body produced the paybook, which looked a bit scarred. Eagerly McVeigh turned the cover open to see the photograph on the inside.

"That's a queer do," he said finally. "Now we'll never know." For the paybook had been pierced and the photograph had no head. . . .

A few days later, I was discussing the situation with Len, when a message came down to us from H.Q., which Len read, then passed over to me. It was quite brief:

"German tanks proceeding in this direction from area Troarn." I felt a chill on my spine.

"What are we going to do?"

Len looked at me.

"Not much we can do, is there?"

"Well, if they come this way, we've just about had it then!"

Len nodded. "Just about."

Against tanks we could do little or nothing. If one

straddled our track, it would wipe out the whole bunch of us, without our being able to do anything much about it. It would be an unpleasant finish.

Len shrugged and said: "We'd better get the sergeant-major and get *something* organized.

The sergeant-major arrived, read the message, and said: "Christ, I'd better load another magazine for my Colt. What're we goin' to do, sir? If there's more than five, we're done, because we've only five Piat bombs."

Len looked at the stocky figure in front of him and laughed. The sergeant-major knew as well as we did, how serious the situation could become, but it was typical of the man that he should not in any way show it.

"You'd better get some sort of ambush prepared, Sarnt-major," said Len, and the sergeant-major bustled off.

We could hear the voice of Taff Edwards detailing various men for various tasks in the ambush scheme, we could see figures scrambling about in the trees and hedges, and a few minute later the sergeant-major reported: "Ambush party present, sir. All ready."

As we went round, he explained his scheme. Everything hinged on the Piat mortar, the only weapon in the troop which was capable of doing any damage to armour. As the tanks came along the track—it was immaterial from which direction—the Piat would engage the leading one from very close range, and from a concealed position. This would halt the leading tank, which, as the turret opened, would then be engaged by men up nearby trees. The following tanks, which would be unable to see what was going on in front, would be engaged by the main ambush party, who would leap from positions behind the wall and up trees on to the tanks themselves, and would cram phosphorous grenades into any openings they could find, preferably the air intake. This done, they would then slide with all possible speed into the nearest slit-trench or ditch.

When the phosphorous grenades had made the tanks uninhabitable the crew would be forced to come up for air, and would then be knocked off by the remainder of the

117

troop, who would still be lurking behind the wall or in their concealed positions.

"The beauty of the 'ole thing," said the sergeant-major earnestly, "is that there isn't a man left out!"

Just then another runner came down the lane leading from H.Q. and handed over a message to Len. He looked at it and began to laugh. It read: "Ref. last message. For *German* read *Sherman*."

It was not until months later that I learned from a man I knew in a wireless intercept unit, that enemy tanks had in fact approached in our direction on that day, but had turned off towards Troarn when about a mile from our position.

Mortaring was the bane of our existence all through Normandy. At every mealtime almost without fail, an odd bomb would whine over and crash down somewhere in the unit area. Sometimes they would put over a sudden concentration, sometimes a series of single bombs, spread out over a period of perhaps two hours, long enough to make sure that the food would be ruined in the particular area where the bombs were falling, and there was always the chance that the first bomb would get a few of the men around the petrol cooker, above whose roaring the whine of the descending bomb could not be heard.

But night time was the favourite, for all types of bombardment. The sun would go down, the mosquitoes would render it impossible to sleep for the first hour or two after dark, and then the first of the enemy guns would start to poop off in the distance.

To the sentry standing by the tree inside the Wall position, the thing always seemed to have an unreal atmosphere at first. Leaning motionless on the Wall, knowing that he was invisible against the background of the tree behind him he watched the outline of the wood opposite become blurred and indistinct, listened to the frogs in the stagnant pool begin their raucous evensong, which helped to accentuate the stillness that took such a hold on the world that it was almost a tangible thing. Sounds which would not have been heard in the daytime were now distinct. Over on the right, from somewhere near Bréville, a burst of machine-gun fire would be followed by the inevitable Very lights, and silence would again take possession, an uneasy silence, in which sentries on both sides stood tensed and listening, suspicious of every sound, natural or unnatural, which jarred upon the stillness. The first stars began to gleam palely in the cold sky above, beginning their turn of duty, and then in the distance, the whole sky would flicker and light, and seconds later the boom of the gun would come to the ears of the watching sentry.

"That railway gun again, I s'pose." Counting, he heard the whine of the enormous missile pass overhead, and after about eleven seconds the rumble of the explosion. A pause, then another from the same compass bearing. Having checked the bearing, he would phone it through to H.Q. and wait for the next gun to start. As each of the sentries sent in their observations, the I.O. could cross-check them and pin-point the gun itself. The information was then passed to the gunners, and if they considered the target important enough they might sling a few back.

Sometimes across the broody silence of the woods there came the sound of tracked vehicles, and after a space of time, a self-propelled gun would open up with its vicious crack, fire a few rounds, and then move to another position. These were almost always 88-mm. guns, which we detested, as there was very little warning of the approaching shell, because the high velocity of the weapon sent the shell with such speed that it could be heard for only about a second and a half before it actually arrived. The damage caused to a position with head cover was negligible, but the effect on the nerves, especially if there was any sort of concentration of fire was considerable. They were, however, not a regular evil, only a spasmodic one.

After this shelling had ceased, or if no S.P. guns were active, after the long-range weapons had delivered their nightly ration of hate, the mortaring invariably began. This was an entirely different and more personal affair, between the units directly facing one another. By this time after their repeatedly unsuccessful attacks, the enemy were fully aware of the dispositions of the troops of the Commando, and were therefore able to bring down extremely accurate concentrations of mortar-fire on our positions, and the Wall position, being perhaps the most accessible, was with unfailing regularity plastered for an hour or so each night. It become a routine, and although the noise was earsplitting, the effect was mainly to prevent anyone from having much sleep, and in the long run, might make a few unfortunates go slightly bomb-happy.

There were several variations of the routine, all designed to have the most wearing effect on the nerves. They might rain bombs down for a period of about half an hour, then stop altogether for an hour, by which time men were settling down to sleep. Then a single bomb at regular ten-minute intervals for about another hour. Another pause, and then the heaviest concentration of the night for perhaps fifteen minutes. By this time there was probably only about an hour or less left till dawn stand-to. And another sleepless night had gone.

News began to reach us of our wounded. We heard from little Ginger Cunningham, our medical orderly, who had been wounded beside me on the beach, yet had struggled along to the battery, then all the long road inland, to treat the other casualties, before he had been evacuated a couple of days later. The hospital report about him arrived, stating that he had been treated for gunshot wounds in both legs and also a broken kneecap. We recommended him for a D.C.M., but without success.

Old Donkin wrote, enclosing a photograph of himself surrounded by attendant nurses, and looking extremely pleased with himself, while the caption underneath the photograph informed the world that "He knew his friends would carry on where he had left off."

We had news of one Churcher, a signaller who had not been long with the troop, and who had been wounded in the battery on D-day. He had been unfortunate before D-day in falling foul of Len on an exercise when his set had gone wrong at a critical moment. He had taken his "rocket" very much to heart, and when he was wounded in the wrist while crossing the beach on D-day, he said nothing, bound it up with his field dressing, and carried on. We reached the battery, where he was with Peter's section, and when they reached the far end of the battery, as he panted along, holding his set with both hands against his chest, a bullet passed through one hand, smashed the set, and went through the other hand, smashing that too. Ignoring the fire which was hissing about him and paying no attention to his hands, he went up to Len, stood to attention in front of him, and said: "Excuse me, sir, I'm sorry, but the set won't work." He was evacuated to England, and later invalided out of the Army, having lost the use of one hand. We recommended him for an M.M. but without success.

Then suddenly we had news of David Haig-Thomas, whose task it had been to act as liaison officer between the Airborne and ourselves. Little Ryder, who had gone to the Airborne as David Haig-Thomas's runner, and who had dropped with him in the night of the 5–6 June, arrived back in the unit. They had dropped according to plan, but had been a bit astray when they dropped, and the whole stick landed in a bog and swamp. Struggling clear of their parachute equipment, it had taken them three hours to get out of the quagmire on to a solid footing, and this had made them behind schedule. To make up for this they had put on the pace towards the R.V. which had been arranged, and had used roads, where, had they had time, they would probably have kept to the fields. They then ran into a German patrol, which was in position behind a hedge, the patrol had hurled out stick grenades and David, who was leading, had fallen soundlessly to the ground. The others went to ground in the ditch, and after a time the medical orderly with them crawled out to where David lay. Although it was dark and there were still enemy about, he made a quick examination and on his return to the others told them David was dead. The approach of another enemy patrol made them pull out and continue by an alternative route.

Later they had met up with some Canadian paratroopers, with whom they remained for the ensuing hectic days. Finally, when the battle had sorted itself out a bit, Ryder had made his way back to No. 4 and there made his report again.

It seemed impossible to believe that a chap like David Haig-Thomas, who had been so happy-go-lucky and so full of the joy of living had gone that way, killed by a stick grenade, chucked out more or less at random from behind a hedge, and the more we all thought about the thing, the more likely it seemed that the medical orderly had in the darkness been mistaken, and that David was wounded and a prisoner somewhere. He had arrived in the unit when it was stationed in Winchester, and had been heralded by his reputation as an oarsman. Apparently he had rowed three times for Cambridge—a feat accomplished by only six men in all, of whom one had been his father—and then for Britain.

The first sight most of them had of him was on a cadre course for which he was detailed immediately he arrived. The whole course was drawn up in battle order on the square for the early morning inspection, when a figure appeared carrying a mass of web equipment over his arm, grinning cheerfully on all and sundry and asked:

"Does anyone know how this bloody stuff goes together?"

That was his first public appearance, but he very soon became known. He was sent to "C" troop, under David Style, because apparently he was a keen climber as well as being an oarsman. This fact was soon the talk of the town, as a result of an escapade he carried out about a week after he came to the unit. His fondness for climbing was not restricted to the normal rock and mountain type, but also to buildings, and while he had been at Cambridge he had scaled most of the buildings in the town at some time or another. So when he arrived at Winchester and noted its cathedral, it was only natural for him to feel the old urge coming over him, and he had succumbed without much of a struggle.

Unfortunately he had been seen while engaged on the climb, and the matter was reported to the C.O. by the horrified bishop, who simply knew that some horrible Commando soldier had desecrated his cathedral by climbing all over it. Lovat, who knew of David's penchant for that sort of thing, sent for him, taxed him with the offence, to which he readily admitted, and sentenced him to go and have tea with the bishop and apologize for his misdemeanour.

That was the end of that.

The next aspect of his character that became known to the unit was the fact that for three years he had explored Greenland, where he had lived with Eskimos, taken photographs and studied birds with Peter Scott. He had a whole collection of slides and gave the unit one or two talks on the subject of his stay there. We found that he was a very amusing and entertaining lecturer and his lectures became very popular with the troops. One way and another he was the most talked-of man in the unit.

When they went down to Falmouth he shook his troop even more by taking them out along the sea-shore and pointing out to them the different types of seaweed and whatnot that were edible. The crowning moment came when he scooped a couple of limpets from a rock and consumed them like oysters, with every appearance of relish. Very few of them accepted his invitation to try one.

The longer he was with the unit the more likeable he became. He was ready to try anything, and had such a fund of varied knowledge that there were few subjects and fewer aspects of life about which he could not speak with some authority. The study of birds was, however, his absorbing interest and hobby. He would lie for hours trying to get photographs, with remarkably good results, and while thus engaged he would forget everything else. He cheerfully claimed to be the only man who had failed to sit his finals at Cambridge through forgetting to turn up, and regarded his excuse of being engrossed in watching two birds by the river as being perfectly legitimate.

Perhaps the most engaging side of his character was his obvious enjoyment of life. He even enjoyed the Army, which was the more surprising as Army life was the one for which he was least equipped, no matter how hard he tried. As time went on, however, he became convinced that the Commando had smartened him up considerably. This conviction was shattered by his small son when David went home on leave. David asked the youngster what he wanted to be when he grew up, and the boy said: "A soldier."

David preened himself.

"Like Daddy?"

But the answer came back with youthful honesty:

"No, I want to be a real soldier."

So David had come back to the unit a sadder and wiser man, and had reconciled himself to the fact that Nature had not intended him to be a soldier.

Cheerful, likeable, generous, forgetful, an unconventional soldier—he was all these things, but he was a man who in his thirty-five years of life had seen more and done more than do most men in their allotted span of three-score years and ten. And the troops, with that discernment and good judgment peculiar to British troops, had respected his achievements, laughed at his military oddities, admired his spirit, and would have gone with him anywhere.

Gradually the whole unit began to believe that he would turn up somewhere, and would come back, as cheerful and full of beans as ever.

As sniper officer I was fortunate in being able to go out with the various snipers in turn, which gave me a certain amount of exercise, a certain amount of excitement, and a way of relieving the exasperation we all felt at having to sit and be mortared day and night without personal reply. It was also useful in other ways.

Since we landed, we had lived, or existed, on the notorious Compo rations, which are no doubt excellent from the medical point of view, in that they supply the nutrition sufficient to keep men alive over a period of time, but which undoubtedly become extremely tedious to the palate. It was felt by the whole troop that it was high time something was done about it, and it was just then that the snipers discovered the calves.

I had been out with Spearman, a very steady Grenadier Guardsman, in the area of Longuemere farm, a deserted farm building about eight hundred yards from "F" troop's lines and about two hundred yards from the main Gonne-ville road along which the enemy had their positions. The farm was used by both sides as an O.P. for a mortar or artillery shoot, and, as it rather dominated the surrounding area, it was useful to the snipers as a central sort of base from which the pairs could operate. Consequently they had to make a fairly careful recce of the buildings and adjoining outbarns each time they went out.

On this particular occasion Spearman and I, on our return to the farm, where we made an exhaustive search of the buildings, had found a number of young calves in a byre. Spearman cast a ruminative eye over them and then looked at me.

"They'd come in handy, wouldn't they?"

I nodded, and the idea was born.

When we reached the troop lines, and made our report, I cunningly suggested to H.Q. that it might be advisable, the next time the snipers went out, to take a protective screen of one sub-section as far as the farm, "to cover the snipers' return to the farm after their patrol." All unsuspecting, H.Q. agreed to the proposal, and the next day four snipers went out, accompanied by half a dozen stalwarts from Sergeant Graham's sub-section. The approach to the farm was carried out with extreme caution, and when it was found to be clear, the snipers took up good positions in the roofs of the various buildings, while the others began to search for the calves. Several were seen in the orchard beyond the farm, which was annoying, as this orchard was under direct observation by the enemy, and it was unwise to move too freely into the open.

So while Carlin tried to cajole the recalcitrant calves back from the orchard, the others contented themselves with a more thorough search of the farm buildings. About half a dozen chickens were raised and pursued round and round the yard, without any noticeable success, three or four pet rabbits were coaxed forth and despatched, but still there was no further sign of any calves, although an enormous barrel of cider was tapped in one outhouse. Then, wandering round the dairy I suddenly came upon three reasonable-sized calves huddled in a dark corner. I nipped outside and called to McVeigh, who had the rope, and the fell work began.

"You open the door, sir, while I get in, then keep it shut till I give you a shout."

He slid into the dairy, and I slammed the door to. There was a frantic scuffling inside, punctuated by numerous oaths in outspoken Lancashire, then McVeigh's urgent voice:

"Open the door."

As I eased the door open, I was hurled backwards into a heap of manure, and a maddened steer, with a rope round its neck, and McVeigh dangling at the end of it, shot forth into the yard and careered wildly in one direction after another. McVeigh hanging on with desperate determination, was first of all thumped resoundingly against the stone wall of the adjacent shed, then dragged on his back across the cobbled courtyard as the beast headed for the gap at the opposite end. Seeing the danger, one of the others leapt into the breach in front of the animal, waving his arms and jumping up and down. This caused the brute to swerve even more violently in the opposite direction, and McVeigh, still at the end of the rope, described an almost perfect arc in the air and finished up with a squelching plomp in a huge pile of refuse and manure, evil-smelling as only a French midden can be.

As though satisfied, the calf came to a quivering stand-still, while McVeigh, gibbering with rage and reeking to high heaven of all sorts of things dragged himself clear of the clinging slime, to come face to face with his particular friend Notman, who was leaning against a cart guffawing with delight. With murderous intent, McVeigh bore down upon him, and the calf might have been forgotten in the ensuing battle, had it not made a sudden move toward freedom.

Fortunately, those who had been onlookers in the previous rodeo display by McVeigh now roused themselves to action and the beast was brought to a standstill, without further casualties. A hasty consultation was held, in which we decided that it would be easier to get the brute home dead than alive, an opinion with which McVeigh was in complete agreement.

Without further delay, it was killed, and we agreed to slaughter one of the others in the byre without bringing them out at all.

Next we had to find some way of carrying the spoils away, as a calf, however small, is heavy, and it was a hot day. Looking round, we soon found a cart, and underneath it lay a huge sheep.

"Mutton's nice," said McVeigh, still full of the lust for blood, "and anyway it looks as though this beast's been there 'undreds of years. It looks old, an' it'd be a pity to leave it 'ere to die all on its own."

With a marked lack of the respect due to one of its age, we dragged the venerable sheep from under the cart, and the knife again did its deadly work. The cart was then pulled clear, and the carcases loaded aboard. We picked up our weapons, wiped the sweat from our brows, and prepared to withdraw.

This was not such a simple matter, because the cart was large and unwieldy, and obviously could not be pushed or pulled through the hedge through which we had made our way to the farm. There was one track leading out to the road which ran from the enemy lines to ours, and at one point, this track was in full view of the enemy forward positions. The route we had used in the approach to the farm had been in a dip, and therefore out of sight.

"Look," I said, "tell Spearman we're going flat out as far as the road. The snipers can cover us that far, then we'll drop off a couple of chaps to cover the snipers coming over, while the other four bash on with the cart along the road. Then when the snipers have got to us, we can use them to cover the rear all the way along, and the rest of us keep the cart going as fast as possible. We'll have to hurry, because they're bound to hear the cart going along this track, and then their mortars'll catch us on the road."

As we manoeuvred the cart to the gateway leading on to the track, Spearman was told of the plan for the withdrawal, and when he had signified his understanding, we began the clattering way to the road. As we neared the exposed part, we quickened the pace to a run, and hurtled across the gap to the road. There I dropped off with the two hindmost men and covered down the road and across the orchard, while the remaining four sweated on with the cart. Then Spearman and his two henchmen left the cover of their roofs and doubled over the open towards us, and when we reached the road, we all five backed up it as far as the first corner, then turned and fled along till we caught up with the cart. We kept up the pace for another couple of hundred yards, then slackened off to regain breath.

McVeigh waxed jubilant. "What'll we have for breakfast in the morning, chops or kidneys? Wait till the troop see this lot. The skipper'll be glad to see us, he likes his scoff too. We can skin 'em tonight, and rough it on the rabbits an' things till tomorrow." Then a thought crossed his mind. "We'd better cover them up with something while we go through Three's lines, or the whole Army'll hear where we've been."

So we stopped the cart at the first of the deserted cottages along the roadside and collected a few bundles of faggots of which all French cottages seemed to have an abundant supply, filled the cart up with them, covering the carcases completely, and then continued on our homeward way.

For the next few days we in "F" troop lived like kings. The war seemed to have taken on a less grim aspect. Holiday was in the air.

One afternoon, I was lying in the sun, which was beginning to go down behind the trees, listening to McVeigh idly discussing with some of his section the latest rumour while finishing off the chops they had done for tea, McVeigh suddenly stopped gnawing at the bone, and sat in open-mouthed astonishment, one hand still poised in mid-air clutching the remnants of his chop, and gaping at a huge semi-naked figure who had leapt from a nearby trench. It was Lewington, a former policeman, clad only in his trousers and gym shoes, who was running about waving his arms, leaping wildly in the air, and making frantic lunges as if at some invisible assailant.

"Christ almighty!" said McVeigh. "Look at Lew, 'e's gone slap-'appy. I never thought 'e'd be one to go that way! 'E's the worst I've seen yet. It just shows you, you never can tell."

They watched the gambolling figure reach the other end of the orchard, then with a yell of triumph he made a final dive, and, clasping both hands together, trotted back towards them. As he drew near they could hear him muttering to himself.

"Good God, 'e's dangerous," said McVeigh, "'ey, wot're you on Lew?"

Beaming happily, the big fellow came across, while they eyed him with considerable suspicion.

"It's my father," he explained.

"*Wot?*" said McVeigh, incredulous.

"Yeh, he collects 'em. Butterflies, and this is one he's not got." And he went contentedly on his way.

McVeigh scowled. "To think I was wasting my time feelin' sorry for 'im, an' all 'e was doin' was chasing butterflies. These coppers are all the same. Can't trust one of 'em."

A faint droning made itself heard, and shading my eyes with my hand, I saw the dots of approaching aircraft. As my only aircraft recognition depended on whether they opened fire or not, I turned to the nearest man.

"What sort of aeroplanes are these, Toombs?"

Toombs looked knowledgeable, and screwed up his eyes as he looked at them. Then he looked pleased.

"They're Marauders, sir, that's what they are."

"What do you think, Sergeant Graham?"

"They're Marauders, right enough, sir, lovely jobs."

The planes drew nearer. They certainly looked good against the blue sky, with the sinking sun glinting on their wings. As McVeigh looked at them, he sighed.

"I wish I was an air-gunner. In about an hour they'll be eatin' eggs an' swillin' beer an' talkin' about a wizard prang. Even if they get knocked off, it's not in a ditch or in a bloody trench. It's a clean life they have. Wonder wot poor bastard they're after this time?"

By this time the droning had increased to a steady roar. We could see quite clearly the white recognition stripes on the wings. Then a small black object left the leading plane, followed by another and another.

"Wot the 'ell's them?" said McVeigh, but he was alone, until he heard the screaming whine and threw himself into his trench where I had been for some time. The ground heaved and shuddered to the explosions of the bombs, as the stick straddled the field in front of us. The nearest was about fifty yards away. The whole affair lasted perhaps five minutes, then the planes wheeled, and, graceful as ever, flew towards home.

Grimly McVeigh dusted himself down as he crawled from the trench.

"I s'pose they'll be laughin' like 'ell now at seein' us scatter. They'll tell each other about it in the pub too. I wish I could lay my 'ands on 'em. It'd be bad enough when it's the filthy 'Un, but it's a sight worse when the bastards are supposed to be on our side." He looked at me and grinned: "For a big man you moved a bit sharpish, didn't you, sir? I never saw you go as fast as that before."

I was about to make some suitable reply, when he noticed someone coming across the orchard towards us.

"Hallo, who's this, I wonder."

They all looked round, someone coming from the direction of H.Q. generally meant trouble of some sort.

"He's not one of ours, is he? He's an officer too."

The figure drew near, and as I got up he announced himself.

"My name's Kennedy. I've been sent to No. 4 as M.O. to replace Doc Patterson, so I thought I'd come round the troops and just see where they all are."

"Well, it's just as well to know where to come to collect the bods, I suppose. C'mon and I'll show you round."

We moved off round the various positions, up to the Wall, where Len and the rest of the troop were to be found.

The whole thing was just bad luck. It was a night just like any other, and the mortaring was no heavier than any other, it was just the same as it always was, some closer than others, some not so close, except for one.

He was on "stag" at the time, just like any other night, standing inside the double hedge, and looking out across the field of corn criss-crossed by the trip-flares he had helped to lay. He was on third shift, from two-thirty till four, and everything seemed quiet when he went on. His rifle lay on the parapet of the position handy for immediate use, as were the grenades, which lay, thirty-sixes on the right, phosphorous on the left. The watch was propped in the middle so that the luminous dial showed only on the safe side, and could not be seen by any approaching enemy. He had a blanket draped round his shoulders, as it was cold, and leaned against the rooty bank for support. He was completely motionless, except for his eyes, which roved ceaselessly across the area of cornfield covered by his sub-section. Along on his right, about twenty paces away, he knew another pair of eyes were alert and watchful, and another still figure would be shivering against the cold background of the bank against which he himself was leaning. Time dragged slowly by.

On the other side of the field he could make out the outline of the wood in which the enemy had formed up on the day of the heaviest counter-attacks. He grinned at the memory. That had been a day. Over two hundred and fifty enemy dead had been counted by the Airborne patrol, lying in heaps on the fringe of the wood opposite their one little sector. And there were always more wounded than dead. Since that day they had never put in another attack in strength, they just sat back and mortared.

He could hear the booming of the big railway gun away in the distance, and reflected that it was a good job it never fired at their particular position. A shell that size must be as big as the one the Navy had landed on them, and that was bad enough, one was plenty.

He was a strange chap, this sentry, never so happy as when he was having a good moan, never so amused as when some carefully-made organization came unstuck. Dour and sullen in appearance, he was not the type to make friends easily. And yet he was respected in the troop, the friends he had trusted him and stood by him as he did by them, and as he had been in the troop longer than most, he was accepted as a sort of institution.

At Dieppe, where the unit landed in gym shoes, his had come unstuck in a bog and he had carried out the assault in his stocking soles. His two troop officers had both been killed, Pat Porteous had taken over, and although wounded had led the final charge to the gunpits, where he was wounded again and lost consciousness. On the withdrawal from the battery position, still in stocking soles, this man had helped to carry the wounded officer back towards the beach. The way lay through brambles and wire and undergrowth and the dead weight of the wounded man was a considerable handicap, but swearing and cursing and sweating they brought him down to the boats. By this time the feet of the man in stocking soles were lacerated and bleeding, but he gave them no heed, and concentrated simply on dumping the wounded officer unceremoniously on to the craft with a last round salvo of oaths.

In the normal life of the unit, he was just another "old soldier" type, dodging fatigues and appearing on sport only when detailed. On parade he was spotless, and his cap badge was his only real pride. In the evenings he could be found any time in a corner of his favourite pub dourly drinking "black and tans" and looking the more sullen the more he enjoyed himself.

His was a queerly contrary nature. He would take a delight in running the unit and his own particular troop down all the time when amongst his friends, but just let him hear any outsider even hint that anything connected with No. 4 was wrong and he would hurl himself metaphorically and, if necessary, physically into the fray in its defence.

It was the same sort of thing on training. Whenever he was detailed to do any sort of job that was not a part of the normal routine, or entailed any extra effort, his first reaction was one of apparent resentment, energetically expressed in a flow of bitter curses, of which no one took the slightest notice. Seeing this, he would depart, still swearing, on his task, and would proceed with vindictive energy, to make a thoroughly good job of it.

On a route march, moaning everlastingly at the weight he was saddled with, the state of his feet, the length of the march, the roads, the weather, the pace, the cheerfulness of the men around him, the apparent length of his turn with the Bren, he would nevertheless take Tich Cunningham's extra kit off him and carry that for a spell to give the smaller man a break, although this did not in any way prevent him from calling the same Cunningham everything he could think of for having brought the stuff in the first place.

Prior to D-day, to his vociferous disgust, he was detailed as a flame-thrower carrier. This entailed the burden of a pack-type flame-thrower, capable of a ten-second squirt. It was extremely heavy, and on the preliminary training, running around the countryside with full operational order, he was reduced to a state of seething silence, which lasted as a rule until the end of the march, when he would dump the thing savagely on the ground and unleash a flood of invective at it and at everything else connected with it, his argument being based on the fact that it would work only for "a miserable ten seconds." The fact that the troop found the spectacle of his being beaten slowly to his knees by the crushing weight of the thing over a longish march rather an amusing one, only served to increase his already considerable powers of abusive rhetoric.

When we actually landed, crossed the beach, and made the dash into the town to the battery, he was there, carrying a stretcher in addition to his hated flame-thrower, and when they reached the battery, the nozzle of the thing was smashed by a splinter. He reported to me and I noticed that instead of the stretcher he was now carrying a Bangalore torpedo.

"Where did you get that?" I asked, and the stolid answer was:

"Well, this thing got broken, an' ah thocht ye might need somethin' else instead, so ah picked this up."

And now he stood, a shrouded figure, looking out over the space of ground between him and the enemy, watching the lazy flight of the Very lights over the German lines, and listening to the booming of the big railway gun in the distance. He glanced at the watch. Less than half an hour to go. Then he would have the pleasure of wakening Toombs and telling him that his turn for "stag" had come.

Then he heard the first of them. In the woods on his right front mortar-flashes lit up the whole sky, and the air was filled with sound. This time, instead of sticking to the Wall though, they seemed to be concentrating on the whole of the troop area. The ground shuddered and heaved, while the smell of cordite drifted over the positions. Still the sentry stood, ducking when any seemed too close for comfort, and scanning the open field in front of him in case the mortaring was simply a screen for a swift attack.

For a moment or two there was silence. They seemed to have paused for breath. As he listened, he could hear no cry for help, no call for stretcher-bearers. That meant there were probably no casualties in the troop area at any rate. He looked at the watch. Fifteen minutes to go.

Again the sky flickered and flashed and the whining screams of the bombs rose to a crescendo of hideous noise. All sense of time and space left him. They were getting

134

bloody near now, seemed to be searching the hedge-line. He pressed himself closer to the bank as the field in front of him opened in a red roar. Branches of the hedges were seared and cut above his head, and he was showered with falling earth. A moment's silence, then he heard three quick successive thumps and saw three flashes over the woods, and the whine which started inoffensively enough suddenly worked itself up into a hellish vibrant rushing on top of him. He swung himself down into his trench by the end beam of the roof, and crouched inside. The walls of the trench shook as the first of the three went off five yards away from the parapet, but there was no time to realize it as with a cataclysmic roar the world heaved, rocked and then became stiflingly dark....

That was the last bomb they sent across, and when the noise had died away, the occupants of the next trench, on looking out to see where it had landed, saw a struggling figure, with clothes alight and nerves in shreds, crawling painfully towards their trench. It was the other occupant of the sentry's trench, who could only whisper:

"Get him out, he's still in there."

And so, from the ruins of his trench, they dug him out. The first bomb had been close, the second had crushed the walls of the trench, and as it was doing so the third had struck the branches of the hedge overhead. The splinters had scythed downwards at an angle, some striking and igniting the phosphorous grenades on the lip of the trench, exploding the thirty-sixes, and some had hurtled through the entrance to the trench itself. Only by exploding where it did could this have happened, and it was just bad luck that he was crouching inside the trench with his back to the door.

He was still alive when we dug him out, but only just. And as we laid him gently on his face on the grass of the orchard, and sent for the doc and the ambulance jeep, he whispered jeeringly at us:

"Let me die, ye bastards, let me die, ye're wasting yer time."

And as we lifted him and placed him on the stretcher on the jeep, he died.

In the history of the war it will find no place. To the dispassionate officialdom of the Records Department it would be just another name, just another number. They would see nothing of the night itself, lit by the flickering of the mortars, of the man staying grimly at his post to the last possible moment, when he hurled himself into the trench. They would not hear the dreadful approach of Death, and would not visualize the burning broken trench.

Perhaps it is as well that it should be so. After all it was only one man. But for the man himself, it was the final answer to the big question, the crossing of the divide.

And the whole thing was just bad luck.

CHAPTER VI

If you can force your heart and nerve and sinew,
To serve your turn long after they are gone,
And so hold on, when there is nothing in you,
Except the Will, which says to them, "Hold on!"

KIPLING

JUNE was almost at an end, and as the month drew to a
close, it became known that the unit was going to move,
and not towards home, but to Bréville. From that day
on, sentries on "stag" at night watched to the right, where
the Very lights soared, and the sound of machine-gun fire
seemed so much worse than in our own sector. That was
Bréville. Each night as the mortaring commenced, it seemed
to start over on the right, and only later work its way towards
us in our position. That was at Bréville. When it became
known that a patrol from either No. 3 or No. 6 Commando
had run into trouble across toward the right, the word at
once flew round: "That was at Bréville." It became a sort
of hoodoo.

Then Len and I went across one afternoon to make a
recce of our future abode, and to see the people we were to
take over from. It was a hot afternoon, and as we drew near,
we were met by the unmistakable smell of death, which
hung brooding over the whole village. A singularly cheerful
bloke from the Airborne, however, said reassuringly:

"It's all right, it's not as bad as it smells. We get one S.P.
gun which comes up most days about five in the afternoon
and bashes off a few rounds, and we get mortared pretty
regularly, but nothing really to worry about. Come and I'll
show you round the place."

We moved off, and I was pleasurably surprised to hear a
familiar voice exclaim: "Well, damn me, shure, I'm glad
to see you. I thought you were dead."

I turned, and looked into the grinning countenance of one George McGuinniss of the Ulster Rifles, with whom I had once been on a sniper course.

I grinned back.

"Hallo, George, how's things?"

"Not too bad. What are you doing here? I thought you weren't coming till next week."

"We're not. But we're just having a look to see what sort of a mess you've got the place in before we take over. If you get a brew on, we'll be back in time to drink it before we go back to our own place."

"Shure, that's damn nice of you. How long'll you be?"

"About a quarter of an hour."

We moved off. The village had certainly taken a hammering. First one side then the other had pounded the place until there was scarcely a house standing. Every roof was shattered at the very least, and everywhere there hung the awful sickening smell of the dead. As we went round the area, the cause of this smell was not difficult to find. In the first place, there were numerous cattle lying about the fields distended and horrible, each carcase surrounded by a swarm of loathesome black flies, which rose in a buzzing cloud as we passed, only to settle again as soon as we had gone. There were two broken German S.P. guns standing derelict, their silent guns still menacing, their equally silent crews covered by an inch or two of soil. Ammunition, live and expended, lay scattered everywhere. Stick grenades protruded from the graves of the men who had hoped to use them. It was a depressing place.

We returned to our starting point, where we were hailed by the cheerful George.

"The tea's up, come and get it. What do you think of the place?"

"Not much."

"Well, you'll get used to it, after a week or two."

We stayed for a time, swapping bits of news, then Len said: "Well, we'd better be going. See you sometime next week, I suppose."

"I expect so. Anyhow, so-long just now."

"Thanks for the tea."

"That's okay, you'll have to call on me when we move down into the valley there. I'll have a decent house then."

We left him, and that was the last we saw of him for he was killed the following week as he stood in the doorway of his "decent house," by one stray mortar-bomb.

On the afternoon of 7 July we moved off and marched the mile or so to Bréville.

There the troop layout was somewhat different to that at Hauger. H.Q. was in the biggest house in the village, "F" troop was in reserve, dug in around the village green, and the remaining troops were strung in a semi-circular perimeter round the back of the village, with "C" troop on the left, then "D," "A," and "E" on the right. "B" troop, being the mortar troop, and having to be prepared to support any one of the troops at any time, was in a little wooded area in a central position just behind "A" troop.

The village itself was right on the edge of the slope which ran down to the plains before Caen, standing on the very end of the high ground, and commanding all the roads in the valley below. On the other side, the rolling woods and close country that we had already learned to know and mistrust, stretched away from us as far as the river Dives, a friendly, hateful country of ambush and booby-trap, of apple-trees and sudden death.

During the stay at Bréville, the daylight patrolling was cut down to an absolute minimum, and the snipers were employed instead. There was an orchard about eight hundred yards in front of the unit position, the far side of which was about one hundred yards from the enemy's farthest outpost, and it was the daily task of the snipers to deny the use of this orchard to the enemy, and to prevent his infiltrating round it towards the flank of "E" troop. As this task lasted from dawn till dusk, the strength and endurance of the individual snipers was taxed to the utmost. They had already sustained casualties in the first few days and in the weeks that had followed, and the strength of the section was reduced in consequence to a bare half of its "established" state. Nor was it easy to replace the men who had been lost, for to make a sniper entails more than simply giving a man a rifle with a telescopic sight attached, and there was no way of training fresh men. The only solution was to select a few likely men and send them out in the company of one of the experienced men or the sniper officer and let them gain their experience that way. The fact that snipers' rifles with telescopic sights were short in the unit and the man more often than not had to use his own ordinary rifle did not make much difference, as the close nature of the country normally gave a maximum range of about a hundred and fifty yards or less, but the most worrying thing from my point of view as Sniper Officer was that my trained snipers were being overworked, and that sooner or later the strain was bound to tell.

Each day the area had to be "covered" by the sniper pairs from six in the morning till ten at night, and the only feasible way was to work out a rotating roster for each pair, giving each a period of four hours patrolling per day, and varying the time each day. As far as possible, the pairs would remain the same, and would have a clear day as often as numbers permitted, for it must be understood that these sniping duties were done in addition to the normal routine duties of the troop, and did not relieve them of the onus of guard or sentry-go. Only the first pair out in the morning could be relieved of sentry duties in the foregoing night.

In the first few days in Bréville, the worst part of the sniping duties was the fact that we came under observation almost as soon as we left our own lines, and we were very quickly the target for a mortar "stonk." On the very first day out from the village, I was with Spearman and Ostick, having been told to recce the patrol area and to contact a patrol from the Ox and Bucks, which we would meet in the neighbourhood of a white cowshed some eight hundred yards in front of the unit positions. We went stealthily out along the only exit from our lines, a line of hedgerow round the edge of another fairly open field in front of that, and saw the white of the cowshed in the far corner of the next field. This was the right-hand border of our patrolling area, and farther to the right was the area allotted to the Ox and Bucks. The cowshed was the joining point.

Skirting the field, we made our way to the shed, to be met at thirty or forty yards range by an overpowering stench, the sickening smell of rotting flesh. We staggered closer, and the first thing that met our gaze was a bloated cow, horribly swollen, lying with its legs stiffly pointing skywards. Beside it was the source of the smell, another cow with a huge gaping wound in its side, its rotting intestines exposed to the clouds of flies that hung in buzzing swarms around it. Holding our breath, we moved quickly round the building, without pausing to make the usual careful observation of the next field, at the far side of which was a line of high trees and thick undergrowth. Once in the open, we realized the danger and whipped into the hedge on our right where we found the other patrol, gave them a hurried warning and moved with all speed behind the shed and away to the left along the lee of a protective hedge. We had gone about a hundred yards, practically at a run, when the first bomb came screaming over and crashed down twenty yards from the white shed.

As we lay in the nearest ditch listening to the shriek and thump of the bombs all around the shed area, I looked at my watch.

"It took them about three minutes from the time we went in front of the byre to get this lot across."

"They must have a man permanently up one of these trees in an O.P."

"I hope to Christ they don't switch across this way, because they're just about level with us there."

That thought made us burrow even deeper into the protection of the banks of the ditch. There came a pause, and we waited with tensed muscles and bated breath. Thump, thump, thump. The sound of the mortars came quite clearly to our anxious ears. Then came the shrill whine of the bombs, which to our relief passed overhead and burst in the line of the hedge which was our return route to our own lines. We exchanged glances. Had we gone for home and the safety of our own lines when the mortaring began, we would have been caught in the open by the bombs searching the return route. As it was, we could now return at leisure, or at least after a decent interval, in comparative peace and quiet, having found out two things of use to us in the future: firstly, that the white shed was under observation from the line of trees, and that the enemy mortars were constantly "on tap" to the observer, and secondly it was wise, having brought down enemy mortar fire, to stay out till he had gone over the return route, which he would surely do.

The first few patrols we made from Bréville were all notable for the amount of enemy mortar fire which seemed to result. So much so, that the troops, seeing any of us on the way out, used to take to ground and wait for what they began to regard as the inevitable.

Our own mortars were, however, not inactive, and did some excellent work in neutralizing the fire of the enemy and warming up his O.P.s, so that if the work of the snipers in this stage of the proceedings was not strictly speaking sniping at all, they did at least serve some useful purpose, by reporting on enemy O.P.s and observing the results of our own as well as the enemy fire.

Thus the days passed, with the snipers working over-time, and the unit as a whole staying put.

Then one day, two things of note occurred. The first, a matter of great moment, was that the first supply of Naafi beer and whisky arrived. The second was that "F" troop were detailed to send out a listening patrol of one senior N.C.O. and five men to sit in an enormous bomb crater at the edge of the orchard whose farthest point reached to the enemy forward positions.

The idea was that if we had a patrol there from dusk to dawn, we would have early warning of any attacking force leaving the enemy lines and heading for ours.

When we were warned of the patrol, Len turned to me thoughtfully.

"I don't know that I like sticking chaps out there, when they don't know the ground. They won't be able to get out to it beforehand, and I can't very well send out your snipers again, when they've been out all day."

I looked at him. I saw what he meant.

"All right. I'm not out today, so I'll take them out tonight."

Len looked relieved.

"Good show, Mac. You can take two or three of the N.C.O.s with you this first time, then they'll know the way out and in when they take the patrols themselves. Don't forget though, it's just a listening patrol. I don't want any of you getting ideas about getting prisoners or anything. We don't want them to know we've a patrol out at all.

"Don't you worry, we'll have no hanky-panky. Let's try that beer."

The beer ration worked out at two bottles per man, the whisky was on a more limited scale. We opened the beer with due ceremony. It was nearly all bad.

McVeigh, spitting out what he had not swallowed of the vinegary stuff, hurled the bottle away from him and exploded: "Naafi beer! Trust the bloody Naafi. No Aims, Ambition or Flippin' Interest. I'll bet some bastard's making a fortune out of this lot too."

I said to Len: "I'll not try the whisky till this patrol's over."

"Right," said Len.

I took the patrol out to the bomb crater just at dusk. Visibility was becoming rapidly more and more curtailed but we reached the crater in time to select our positions with the care that on such a job is so necessary. The crater was about thirty feet in diameter and perhaps eighteen feet at the deepest point. The edges of it were humpy and irregular, and one side of it bit into the orchard which we were to keep under observation. It was at this side that I placed the Bren, covering the expanse of the orchard. One man was placed at either side of the crater and one had the task of watching the rear. I lay beside the Bren gunner. The orders were that nobody should under any circumstances move from his position, unless given a direct order to do so by me. If any one of them was certain that he could hear or see something untoward, he was to draw the attention of the next man to it, and I would finally decide whether or not they would pull out to inform the unit, stay and knock off the prowler if there were but one, or simply lie doggo. And so our vigil began.

The first hour seemed endless. The sounds of the day gradually died with the fading light, the horizon closed in, the grey clouds of darkness crept upwards from the top of the line of woods, gradually to envelop the entire sky, while the accompanying surge of silence laid its fearful hush on all the world below. Only the buzz of the swarming mosquitoes could be heard, an incessant humming that seemed to grow the louder as the silence strengthened. The first stars gleamed palely in the anaemic sky, and in their struggle with the dying light above, from which they emerged in the course of time strong and triumphant, there was reflected all the impotence and frailty of mankind, the majestic inevitability of the universe.

Sitting in the crater, I squirmed under the besieging hordes of mosquitoes. I put my hand flat on my face and then drew it slowly downwards. I felt the myriad bodies under my palm squash and slither. I longed to be able to scratch, to slap the back of my neck, to wriggle clear of the unrelenting foe. The bites they made were sharp and painful, after a time the expectation of each fresh bite was enough to make me wince. It was a refinement of torture from which there was no escape till morning. I almost groaned aloud at the thought. Wearing a face veil was worse than useless, because they always succeeded in getting under it eventually, and then they were even worse than before, as the frantic high-pitched humming they made in their efforts to escape was almost as hard to bear as the bites they inflicted the while.

I forced myself to relax. I wished I'd taken a course of Yogi or something, then I could ignore the things. What was the time. I looked at my watch. Half past eleven. That meant five and a half hours to go. I was beginning to get cramp in my right leg too. God, I was unhappy. In a flood of self-pity I eased myself into a less uncomfortable position. A horse-fly settled on my wrist and bit it about halfway through. I took the beast in my finger and thumb and hoped as I squashed it that I was hurting it as much as it had just hurt me. . . .

Then with a colossal roar the artillery barrage started up behind us, and it came as a relief to all of us, for it gave us something to think of apart from our own discomfort and the mosquitoes. We listened to the shells screaming overhead towards the enemy woods, and then to the sound of the bursts. In the cover of the noise we all took the opportunity of changing position, stretching our limbs into less cramped attitudes, and shifting any loose earth from various places, so that when the ensuing silence did come it would not be broken by the scuffling of cramped movements nor the slithering of loose earth descending to the bottom of the crater.

The barrage stopped as suddenly as it had begun, and Very lights soared up from the enemy lines. In the crater we lay still. The lights were of more use to us than to the enemy because they lit up the whole orchard, and as it was obvious that the Germans would not illuminate any patrol they had just sent out into that area, it was safe to assume that no patrol had been sent out. The Very lights continued and I felt almost happy in the darkness of the crater. It seemed the Hun was jumpy.

Gradually the Very lights died away, and things returned to normal. It was 12.15.

Back in the troop lines, aroused by the hellish din of the barrage, Len and the sergeant-major looked at one another. They were in the ruined cottage we had fitted out as troop H.Q. The two gleaming bottles of whisky sat on the mantelpiece, winking in the candle-light, and rocking slightly with the vibration of the barrage.

"Not much chance of any sleep in this," said the

sergeant-major hopefully. Len wavered. Then the door opened and Gordon Webb, who was now running "C" troop since David Style had been wounded, came in. In his hand was a bottle of whisky.

"You've a patrol out in this, haven't you?" he asked.

Len nodded. "Yes," he said. "Mac's taken them out."

Gordon set his whisky down on the table. "Poor old Mac," he said. "He was a nice chap. We'd better have a drink."

At about a quarter to one, out in the crater, we heard an aeroplane flying fairly low passing overhead. It was followed by another, and then another. We heard no more for the Ack-Ack then opened up and red streaks whipped viciously upwards in the direction of the sound. Shrapnel began to rain down in the trees around us. One bit landed with a dull whew-plomp a few feet from the edge of the crater. Searchlights began to sweep the skies and through some freak of reflected light, the Bren gunner, Burrell and I on the far edge of the crater from the flickering lights, saw to our horror our own shadows projected up on to the trees of the orchard. We slid unostentatiously under the rim of the crater, and I made a mental note to remind the next lot about that, as it might be liable to lead to trouble.

The air attack lasted about three-quarters of an hour, then quiet again reigned. The mosquitoes kept up their incessant attack. It seemed as though the night would never end. Then suddenly I stiffened. Along the hedge to my left, in the only blind spot of our position, I seemed to hear a stealthy movement. It was only the suspicion of a sound, but it was enough to make me reach for the grenades I had placed handy on the lip of the crater. I then waited for the approach of whatever was there. The stealthy sound drew cautiously nearer. I leaned over to Burrell and breathed in his ear:

"There's somebody coming along this hedge, I think."

"Ay, ah heard it as well."

"Don't fire unless I say."

"Okay, sir."

146

Another eternity of time then passed, in which the sounds of movement drew nearer and nearer. When they were about fifteen feet away, they stopped, and I had the uneasy feeling that some enormous lout in jackboots and coalscuttle was leering in fiendish delight as he pulled on the cord of a stick-grenade. The suspense became well nigh intolerable. I gripped my thirty-six grenade in my right hand and drew comfort from its cool touch. Another movement. Then another. Two or three more and whoever was there would be in sight, silhouetted against the sky. We waited. Nothing happened. Then I frowned in puzzlement. I could hear breathing. I glanced sharply at my own man on my left, but the tense attitude told me that Sergeant Jones had also heard the sound and was alert. Perhaps the chap didn't know we were there after all. If that were the case, he very soon would. Still we waited for the step that would bring the enemy into view. The breathing at the other side of the hedge continued. Then a slight movement, and something white showed through the branches of the hedge. I felt a prickling down my spine. Another step, and I found myself watching a large and placid white horse move into the gap in front of us. A sharp reaction came over me in a wave and I felt like a piece of chewed string. I imagined the others felt the same way. Silently we watched the horse pick its way across our front, and start its way down the hedge on the right of the orchard. The mosquitoes attacked with renewed vigour.

We settled down again to watch and listen, while the horse, unaware of the tension it had caused, meandered down along the right-hand hedge of the orchard. It began to get cold.

Away on the right, in the Ox and Bucks area, a machine-gun sputtered into life, and the enemy line was again lit up by a succession of Very lights, which shot upwards, hung, broke, and began their slow descent, while unseen eyes searched every shadow and corner. The firing increased, but this time it was mainly German weapons that could be heard. Their higher rate of fire made it easy to recognize them in the darkness, each burst sounding like the tearing of a strip of emery paper. As there was no answering fire, I supposed the Ox and Bucks patrol had been a small one, detailed to recce an area, which they had found to be occupied in some strength. That being the case, they had disengaged rapidly, and would now very sensibly be lying low waiting for the enemy fire to die down before returning to make their report.

In the meantime though, the whole enemy line was coming to life and firing away at nothing in particular. There would be a pause of a few minutes, then another series of bursts and more Very lights. In all this lasted about half an hour. It was just after three o'clock.

In the crater, cold and a mass of bites, we lay, stiffly, concentrating on keeping alert for the last two hours of the eternity that had been the night's vigil. It was difficult to maintain the same mental alertness that we had had at the start of the night. Thoughts kept straying to other things, other places, other people, and a sense of unreality kept creeping in. Even the crater seemed unreal. We would probably wake up and find the nightmare of the mosquitoes had been only a nightmare and not reality. It was the darkest time of the night too. No patrol would come out now. Might as well relax a bit. The night was as good as over anyway, only an hour and a half to go. Then:

"Christ, what's that?"

A sudden rending rattle of machine-gun fire from directly opposite our crater. Very lights shooting upwards, and bullets hissing through the branches over our heads made us duck and cling closer than ever to the friendly soil. Then we caught sight of the white horse careering round the orchard whinnying with fright. It had made its round of the hedge until it had reached the gap in the hedge leading to the nearest enemy position fifty yards farther down. All unsuspecting, it had continued on its peaceful way, till it had been heard by the enemy machine-gun post in the corner, and they, taking it for a patrol, had opened up without waiting to make sure.

148

For the next half-hour, odd shots came whistling over, and odd Very lights still went up. Our main worry was that the enemy might decide to send out a patrol to investigate, and if this patrol was strong enough, finding the orchard unoccupied, it might then decide to stay on there, which would make it more than awkward for us in the crater. Another anxious half-hour followed, and then we could see the first suggestion of the new day in the sky to the east. As we had watched the clouds of darkness overrun the rearguard of the retreating day, so we now watched the new day gradually insinuate itself into the dark folds of the summer night, and as the light became increasingly grey, we left the crater and made our way stealthily, albeit stiffly, along the hedges towards our own lines.

When we reached the centre of the village where "F" troop was, we headed for the cookhouse, where I left the others to wait for the first brew of the day, while I crossed to H.Q. to render my nil report.

This done, I turned my steps towards the troop H.Q. I pushed open the door, and as I struggled through the enveloping folds of the blanket hung across as a black-out, I was greeted by the sound of heavy breathing.

Inside the room, everything was in darkness, and as I groped around for matches to light the candles, my hand brushed over a glass. Luckily the bottle remained intact. Without waiting to find the matches, I pulled down the black-out screen, opened the shutters, and let the morning light stream into the room.

Two heavy heads lifted, and four bleary eyes blinked at me.

"Ismister M'Dougall," said the sergeant-major owlishly.

"He's not dead! I knew he'd come back," Len croaked in delight.

"Then we've 'ad all that worry for nuthin'," said the sergeant-major.

"That's true enough," said Len. He scowled at me. "Don't let it happen again," he said.

They both sank back on their respective couches into

stertorous sleep. I later learned how they had passed almost the entire night swapping yarns while listening to the din outside and wondering how I was faring amongst it.

One morning, about 18 July, we were roused from our slumbers by the usual cannon and machine-gun fire of the Lone Raider as he zoomed down over the village. A series of loud explosions by the house which Len and I shared with the sergeant-major made us dive for cover, and when it was all over, we drifted outside to see what damage had been done.

Along the lane between the houses was a line of gashes in the turf, and a cannonshell had struck the corner of the wall giving on to the street. We surveyed the marks, collected a couple of nose-caps for identification, and were about to return to our abode when we heard a distant droning in the sky and in the cold light of the morning we could see what seemed to be a huge mass of aircraft approaching.

"I say, what the hell's this lot?"

"Can't be the German Air Force, they haven't got that many."

"Let's hope not, anyhow."

"Better find out what they are, just in case. Get a hold of someone who's been on a course."

Fortunately, some of the troop had been aroused by the noise and had appeared to see what was going on, and one of them could be heard saying:

"Look at this lot comin' acrost. Bloody luvly, ainnit? Wot are they, Liberators?"

"Yeh, there must be stacks of 'em too."

By this time the force of aircraft was practically overhead and stretched back as far as the eye could see. More and more seemed to be pushing on from behind, while the whole sky above us seemed to be completely filled with huge majestic monsters which swept on inexorably to their target, as yet unknown to us excited troops below.

As they crossed over towards Caen, flak curved up to meet them but was ignored, as with a sovereign disdain the leading aircraft let loose a stream of marker flares to descend on the doomed town. The flak increased in intensity, and it seemed impossible that some of the tightly-packed mass of planes should not be hit. Even as we watched, awed, we saw one plane stagger, swerve, and burst into flame. For a moment it looked as if it was about to plunge to the earth, but instead it righted itself and continued, burning, towards its objective. From where we were, we could see the bombs leave the stricken aircraft, which then turned, and losing height all the way made for the sea.

After a time the flak, which had at first been active, was swamped by the weight of the attack. One gun continued to fire ineffectively but defiantly for a while, then that too was silenced.

For three solid hours, while the sun rose in the blue sky wave after wave of planes passed over. Liberators and Lancasters, with, away up in the heavens above, a host of protecting Spitfires which came into view only when they swooped down to twist and turn immediately above the main force.

Over the town lay a pall of black smoke, but still they came, and still the bombs screamed downwards. It was little wonder that the enemy troops in the town were reduced in those three hours from the much-vaunted "Iron men" of Germany into a collection of mouthing, twitching creatures, too dazed to know anything but the terror inspired by the avenging rain of death that descended upon them from the sky. Most of those who lived through the air attack and survived the subsequent ground assault will be affected for the remainder of their natural lives. They who laughed in glee at the bombing of Warsaw and Rotterdam laughed no longer.

To us in Bréville it was an inspiring sight and set everyone in a cheerful frame of mind for the rest of the day. As McVeigh put it: "Wot's a couple of mortar bombs beside that lot." It altered the whole perspective of things for us, widened the horizon that for most of us had been restricted to a few hedgerows and an orchard.

That night, those on sentry and on patrol heard the steady rumble of tracks along the road from the bridges. It was a sound that could denote only one thing, the bridge-head across the Orne was finally to be exploited. The sound we had been waiting six long weeks to hear came to us as music, as a welcome harbinger of hope.

In the morning, on the plains stretching away from our viewpoint towards the remains of Caen, we were able to watch the tanks deploy and race off into the mists of the horizon, from which came dully the sound of gunfire. We felt somewhat Napoleonic as we watched from our exalted position the battle unfold across the plains below, and the mortar-bombs that still crashed from time to time into the village or its outskirts, as though to remind us that we were still in the war, were treated with suitable disdain.

Spearman was a damned steady chap; the more I worked with him, the more I thought so. He had sound ideas, too, on working out a sniping patrol, and he took a chance at the right time. We'd covered the ground so often by this time, that we knew just where we were likely to come under fire, or be observed, and so we knew when to crawl and when it was reasonably safe to stand up and walk. We knew which hedges to use and which to avoid, we knew which routes the enemy patrols used to come out from their lines, and we knew where these patrols set up their machine-gun posts, and although the enemy patrolling was restricted chiefly to sending out standing patrols at night, we still took no un-necessary risks as we made our way out on the daily sniping patrols around the area of the orchard.

The afternoon was hot and sunny, and at home the trees would be filled with the movement and song of birds, but here in the fertile wilderness that was Normandy, there were no song birds in the trees or hedgerows, and only an occasional magpie or wood-pigeon flitted uneasily amongst the fruit-trees.

As we reached "E" troop's forward position, we paused to eat a few of the cherries that grew in abundance in the corner of the field. It was a routine, and it was at this point that we usually met the other pair returning at the end of their patrol. This time it was Ostick and O'Connor who joined us. These had been fired on as they worked their way along the left-hand hedge of the orchard by a machine-gun sited in the corner of the orchard. That had been about an hour before and had been one single burst. That was all they had to report.

Spearman and I moved into the thicket that gave on to the open field in front of "E" troop's post. We checked with the men on duty there, to tell them of the proposed movements of the patrol, so that there should be no possibility of being shot up by an over zealous Bren-gunner, and then slipped out into the field. At this point we always walked quite openly, if also quickly, because if we were seen and fired upon, it would be at fairly long range, whoever fired would be visible to the Bren-gunner we had just left, and anyway we had a lot of crawling to do when we got farther out, and crawling is a tiring business.

A few yards in the lead, Spearman was armed with a Colt automatic and a couple of grenades, while I carried a rifle from which the woodwork had been removed. As the rifle had not originally belonged to No. 4 and was not on the unit's books, there could be no Court of Inquiry into this wilful damaging of Government property. The reason for our being thus armed was a result of experience in the close type of country in which we had to operate. Amongst the thick hedges and trees through which we had to pass, we might quite well come face to face with an enemy recce patrol, and in this case the grenades and pistol would be of more use than the rifle, while in the few comparatively open fields, the rifle would be of more use than the close-range weapons.

Quickly we skirted the field and made our way along the hedge towards the end of the field. Here we became more cautious, as we worked our way left in the direction of the orchard. Halfway along this hedge was a gap, which was in reality the entrance to a double line of hedge which ran directly into the enemy positions at the other end of the next field. The lane inside this double hedge was not

153

an open one, and vision was restricted to a few yards, but enemy patrols had used it on occasion to bring up a machine-gun which had then fired on fixed lines throughout the night. So we approached it with considerable care and suspicion before crossing it to reach the corner of the orchard.

We were now beside a rather straggly hedge, at the other end of which was the hedge where Ostick and O'Connor had come under fire. But the other two had gone the other way round into the orchard, and had come up to this hedge from the corner diagonally opposite us.

As we lay in the shelter of the hedge junction, we considered the next move. We had never before gone the length of this particular hedge, because it faded away in the middle, and left a broad and unpleasant-looking gap which we would have some difficulty in skirting. It would mean a crawl of some forty or fifty yards to a clump of shrub near the far end of the orchard, from which we hoped to be able to lie and have a look at the corner of the enemy wood in which the machine-gun post was sited. We would then make our way back the way we had come to a point from which it had on several occasions been possible to get in a shot. After that, we would return home.

That decided, we eased out into the orchard, and made our way slowly and with infinite care along the line of the hedge. The afternoon seemed unnaturally still, every sound was like the crack of doom. We moved by stages, one going forward, the other covering, then slipping forward to join the leader. When we neared the gap we paused in a dip to work out the best route from there, and agreed it would be better to make our way individually to a depression containing a slimy pond, from which we would be able to cover the last stage to the clump of shrubs that was our goal. We would have to crawl all the way to the pond.

From our present position we could see the edge of the enemy wood, but not the corner, and we studied the whole length of it for a good ten minutes or so before separating. There was no sign of movement anywhere amongst the trees that we could see, and so I set out from our friendly dip. I bore slightly to the left, while Spearman remained for a moment in the dip to see if the movement from it had attracted any unwanted attention. Having satisfied himself that there was still no sign of activity along the edge of the wood, he wormed his way out a little to the right, towards an Airborne container that lay half-smothered in the folds of its parachute about twenty yards from him. He moved only when I was still, and remained motionless while I inched my way forward, to reach a log that was my halfway house. There I lay while Spearman wormed over to the container, then, finding that I was hidden from sight of the wood by a patch of hedge, I slipped across the remaining distance to the pond at a crouch, and lay down to recover my breath while Spearman completed the rest of his crawl.

The pond was about fifteen feet wide, and as we sat wiping the sweat from our eyes, Spearman caught sight of something lying in the slime at the other side of the pool. It was a British rifle, twisted and warped, with the stock blown away. Together we went to investigate, and as we neared the far side we could see other articles of equipment lying half-covered by the unpleasant slime. A web belt and bayonet, the cross-straps, and finally a filthy field dressing, clotted and stained. Silently we looked. Then Spearman's lips framed the words:

"Wonder where the bloke is?"

I shrugged. I had a feeling we would find out soon enough.

"Let's get on."

We peered cautiously out to the clump of bushes, which was about forty paces away, half-right.

"Looks as though we'll have to crawl the whole way." I started off. By the time I had reached halfway, I was dripping with sweat, and as I lay face downwards in the grass, my nostrils were assailed by the brooding sickening stench of death. It is a smell that can never be mistaken, and I began to search around for the cause, but could see nothing. I pushed on towards the shrubs, and the smell grew worse as I neared them. Ten paces short, I waited till Spearman was beside me. I could scarcely stand the smell, and could see that Spearman was not enjoying it either. We crawled the last bit together till we were at the edge of the little mound on which the shrubs grew in a tangle. A log lay in our path and as I slithered my body over it, I felt something round roll out from beneath my hand. I glanced sharply down, and my stomach retched and heaved. I shut my eyes and swallowed, desperately trying to prevent myself from vomiting. I had put my hand on an Airborne helmet, in which there still remained clotted the ghastly remnants of a head.

Spearman, who had been looking ahead, now turned and saw the helmet.

"Christ," he said, "there's three bodies out there as well."

I crawled quickly past the helmet and looked. The three bodies lay in the open, where they had fallen on the morning of D-day. They had obviously been caught by a machine-gun covering down the gap in the hedge, as they had tried to make their way to the container, and there they had lain ever since, while the enemy sat and doubtless hoped that someone would come and try to bury them. Beyond them was another clump of brush behind which was the gap where the other two snipers had been seen.

To remain where we were was out of the question. The afternoon was hot, what breeze there was, was coming towards us, and it was all we could do not to be sick.

"Let's get out," I said. We looked round. Behind us, deeper in the orchard, the trees were thicker and there was a fair amount of broken branches and brushwood lying about or dangling from the trees; the cover was sufficient to make us a very difficult target.

"If we run like hell from here we can get behind that lot, and work our way round from there."

"Right."

"Come on, then."

Together we rose and streaked for the cover of the trees.

This gained, we trotted quickly across the orchard, keeping to the thickest parts, until we reached the far hedge. There we sat for a few minutes in the ditch till the feeling of nausea wore off. We still had two hours to go, and so we worked round the edge of the orchard, back across the gap leading down to the enemy line, and into the hedge at the other side. From here we wormed our way into a position in the cross-hedge, where, lying in the ditch amongst the brambles and roots, we had a clear view across the field, at the other side of which was the hedge forming the enemy line.

In this hedge were numerous gaps, and on several previous occasions, one or other of the snipers had been able to get in a quick shot as some unsuspecting German moved along from one position to another. Since then, the enemy had become much more wary when moving about, and usually remembered to run across the gaps, and as these were not very wide, it was now seldom that a good shot was forthcoming.

So we lay and waited, while the mosquitoes settled on us in droves. It was by now mid-afternoon, the sun was high and blisteringly hot, there was a shimmering haze on the ground, and a soft summer breeze curled lazily across our front. The hum of insects was the only indication of life. Neither of us spoke, and half an hour went by. Then a figure in field-grey dashed across the last of the gaps in the hedge opposite. Another followed. They had been visible only for a fleeting second and it would have been senseless to risk a snap shot, which would inevitably have brought answering mortar fire down on or around our position. Shooting was worth while only if a hit were certain.

Another interval of silence. Then to my astonished ear came the sound of soft whistling, as though through closed teeth. It seemed so close as to be right beside me. I turned and glanced at Spearman, who lay on the other side, and found him looking at me in some surprise, and a certain disapproval.

"Was that you whistling, sir?"

I shook my head, and pointed to the left.

157

"It must be somebody in that hedge," I breathed.

Spearman looked startled.

"Well, he must be near."

We waited, straining our ears for some further indication of the intruder's presence, but none was forthcoming, nor was the whistling repeated.

"We'd better have a look at that hedge," said Spearman, "or else the bastard might get us as we're pulling out."

"All right."

"Well, if you cover me till I get into the ditch at the back, then come across, we can start out from there."

Without waiting for an answer, he slipped out of the back of our ditch and wriggled over into the other one. For a moment or two he disappeared, then he again came into view and beckoned me over. When we were both in the ditch, we lay for several minutes searching the hedge for some sign of any hidden enemy, without success.

"How are we going to do this?" said Spearman. "Are you going to cover me from here?"

"No, if I stay here and you get hit, I won't see what's hit you. We'd better get to the gap together, and then see what happens when we get there. There can't be more than one or maybe two, or we'd have heard them."

"Well, I'll stay a couple of paces in front, because a pistol's handier than a rifle, and I'll have a grenade as well."

We pulled ourselves clear of the ditch, crossed quickly and silently to the other hedge, and crept to the gap. When a few yards short, Spearman dropped to the ground and crawled to the fringe, while I stood close to the hedge a few paces behind him. Tensely we listened, then Spearman signed that he was going to nip across the gap, and I moved up to take his place. He flitted across, and we both waited for the burst of fire from the lane. None came.

For the next fifteen minutes we made a thorough search of the hedge and the near part of the lane, and found no trace of anyone.

"That's bloody queer," I said. "We can't both have been mistaken."

158

Uneasily we returned to the place where we had been lying. Both of us were a bit on edge at the unsatisfactory ending to the episode, and we both had the feeling that things were not as they should be. We lay for about a quarter of an hour without hearing or seeing anything, although every nerve was taut, and every sense alert.

"I wonder if we should have a look farther down that hedge."

"We can if you like, sir."

"Come on then."

The silence was oppressive, and I began to ease myself out of the ditch, when the air was rent by the scream of shells passing overhead, and all the length of the enemy hedge-line a series of black puffs of smoke appeared above the trees. With the bursts, fragments hissed and crackled through the hedge in which Spearman and I were crouching.

"That's our artillery," I said.

"These are airbursts," said Spearman.

"Let's get to hell out of here."

We threw caution to the winds, jumped out of the back of our ditch through the other hedge, and tore down the hedge leading into "E" troop's listening post. We hurtled past the Bren-gunner, and stopped only when we had reached the cluster of cherry-trees. There we sat down, and Spearman lit a cigarette. I looked at my hands. They were trembling almost uncontrollably. I got up and broke myself a branchful of cherries.

"Thank God, it's my day off tomorrow," said Spearman. "Much more of this an' I'll be going slap-happy."

I looked at him.

"When I tell H.Q. that the chaps are getting worn down, they turn round and say 'Worn down? But judging by the nil reports that you send in, nothing ever *happens*.'"

I spat out a cherry stone.

"We'd better go home an' have some tea."

On 31 July the unit moved to the area of Bois de Bavent. This move was wholly unexpected, and was not particularly

popular, for the Bois de Bavent had a singularly evil reputation amongst the men of the Airborne, whose various
units had held it all along. They had christened it the
"Burma Road" because the reverse slope of the hill, which
was the only approach route to the actual positions which
was invisible to the enemy, was an unpleasant mixture of
thick low scrub, tall trees and dry dust. Hung on trees all
over the place were notices saying: "Go Slow. Dust Draws
Fire"; "Go to Hell if you will, but Go Slow"; "Go Slow—
It's all right for you, but we've got to Live here," and many
other variations of the same theme. At the top of this slope
was a metal road, which came under extremely accurate
shell- and mortar-fire any time a vehicle chose to take the
risk and thundered along it, and very frequently at odd
times when there was nothing on it at all.

The troop positions were beyond this road, in the field
adjoining it, most of them being at the far side, on the edge
of the wood. The enemy were in this wood, rarely attacked
in any strength, and mortared incessantly. So close were
they to the forward listening posts, that the men in these
posts could hear the plomp of the mortar-bomb being put
in the barrel of the mortar. As soon as this was known, it was
arranged that the men on duty listening posts should be
equipped with whistles and as soon as they heard the plomp
they were to blow the whistle so that the others farther back
should have some warning. It was thought that this would
save unnecessary casualties.

It was into this brooding gloom that Guy Vourch
returned on 6 August, after hounding hospital staffs in
Guildford, Wolverhampton, Lichfield and Beaconsfield to
let him out. Throughout the two months of his treatment
and subsequent recovery, he had been in a ferment of
anxiety about the unit and his own troop in it. From his
young brother he heard scraps of news, but a grubby field-
postcard never said much, so that his imagination was left
to fill the many gaps. He was shocked at the change he saw
in the whole unit. Gone was the exuberance of the early
days. Gone too was the elastic spring of physical fitness. He

found men who were nervy, tense, men who seemed to be listening over their shoulder all the time, as indeed many were doing.

Casualties were at the level of one or two per day, which had become a constant drain on the strength of the unit. The irritating thing was that it now seemed to be the old, experienced men who were being hit. Everyone in the Commando was becoming increasingly jumpy. It was obvious to all of us that unless something happened fairly soon, none of us would be in a fit state to put in the attack that would clear the enemy from the woods this side of the River Dives. Yet we all knew that sooner or later, that was what we would have to do.

The dusk stand-to came to an end in a cloud of mosquitoes at about 10.30, and no sooner had we settled ourselves down for the night than aircraft started to drone overhead. At night German planes never seemed to make their attack as soon as they came over, but they would drone menacingly to and fro, backwards and forwards, round and round in the darkness above, while we below waited for the whine of the falling bombs. This time these did not at first materialize, and the wise ones decided that the planes were there only for reconnaissance, and therefore nothing would come of it, As though to support this theory, the Ack-Ack did not do much in the way of shooting either, and after an hour or so, the planes throbbed their way out of earshot altogether. Relieved, we all dropped off, only to be wakened after a quarter of an hour by thrumming planes, the roar of the Ack-Ack, the whine of the bombs, and the shuddering crash of the explosions.

Wearily, I lay in the foot of my narrow home, and tried unavailingly to shut out the noise from my mind. The walls of the trench kept shaking with every bursting bomb that fell within a quarter of a mile. I was afraid, as I always was when a bombing attack was in progress. I loathed the idea of being crushed and smothered in a trench, but to give in to my natural instincts and go and wander about outside would do no good, I'd only become as bomb-happy as one

161

member of the troop already was, and be an even greater menace all round, as well as losing the last remnants of self-control that I possessed. A plane came in low, and the noise of the Ack-Ack reached a new pitch of ear-splitting venom. Every individual bang made my head throb and ache. I found that my hands were clenched tight, and every muscle in my body was taut. I forced myself to relax, stretched my limbs, and tried to pretend that I was in bed at home and the noise I heard was just thunder. The plane came back in a furious rush, and this time I heard the shrill scream of the descending bomb. I bunched up and waited for the end, for the sound was right on top of me. There was a heavy thud, and the whole trench shook and shuddered. Little dribbles of earth fell on me from the roof, but there was no explosion. I hoped it wasn't delayed action, that would be the last bloody straw. I tried to pray, but as I couldn't think whether it would be better to have a quick death or to go on living, I gave it up, and lay listlessly listening to the inferno of noise about me.

It finished quite suddenly, and the comparative silence pressed on my eardrums almost as painfully as the noise had done. After a while of waiting for something else to happen, I decided that perhaps they'd finished for the night after all, and began to think of sleep again.

Then the barrage burst upon me, and I groaned aloud. Through the gas cape covering the door to my trench I could see the flickering all over the sky. The noise of the guns was, if anything, worse than before. I covered my ears with my hands, but it was no use. There was no answering fire of any sort, but the guns kept hammering on. I tried to concentrate on something else, and found myself repeating out loud the lines from Homer:

> O friends be men, and let your hearts be strong,
> And let no warrior, in the heat of fight
> Do what may bring him shame in others' eyes.
> For more of those who shrink from shame are safe
> Than fall in battle, while with those who flee
> Is neither Glory, nor reprieve from Death.

162

I reflected bitterly that Homer hadn't to cope with the racket that was going on now, and the thought seemed to do me good. Yet I felt that the lines applied to me, and tried even harder to get outside myself, and think of something other than what was going on around me. I thought desperately of various cricket matches I had played in, selected one, and went through it ball for ball, and over for over. I thought of Goldenacre, with the slight slope running down from the red pavilion towards the even smoothness of the square where the stumps were pitched, the slope that made a running catch in the outfield so difficult. I thought of the toil I had put in night after night at the nets, of the slip-cradle which so often had made my hands raw and sore, in the early April days, when the frost was still on the ground. I wished I could be there now.

The barrage stopped. Gratefully, I looked at my watch, it was two o'clock. Dawn stand-to was at 5.15. Surely nothing else would happen now.

As if to give me the lie, a mortar bomb burst in the wood in front of troop H.Q. More followed, falling mostly about a hundred yards either to right or left. Then bursts of machine-gun fire rattled above the general din. I listened, and decided that it was probably only a patrol out spraying about in the general direction of the troop, they might even be firing on fixed lines. There was no answering fire, so it couldn't be any sort of attack. I noted that I no longer felt the same sweating fear that I had experienced in the air attack, and reflected that it was probably the psychological reaction to the knowledge that, if they were near enough to fire a machine-gun at me, I was near enough to fire back at the machine-gunner, and my trench was mortar-proof.

The mortaring died down, but the machine-gunning continued. I heard a scrabbling at the door of my trench, and a head appeared against the sky. It was the bomb-happy member of the troop.

"What's the matter?" I said shortly.

"Sir, the patrol's cut off."

The patrol was a listening patrol of two men, about two hundred yards forward of the main troop position. If they were cut off, it meant the enemy had infiltrated into the edge of the small wood, and were therefore as near as a hundred yards. It was most unlikely that they could get as close as that without being heard by the patrol. I looked at the bomb-happy one. The man was trembling visibly, and his head turned continuously to cast furtive glances over his shoulder. His breath came in whistling gasps that were almost sobs. The extraordinary thing was that he was more or less normal by day, and resented any reference to his apparent lapse of the night-time. I thought I'd better go and see what was going on, so heaved myself out of the trench.

It was a clear starlit night, which made the possibility of enemy infiltration even less likely. The machine-gun fire which was still going on, seemed to be coming from the place where they usually fired on fixed lines, and the bullets were swishing at a safe height overhead. There certainly was no sign of anything as close as a hundred yards threatening the troop, and I turned to the man.

"How is the patrol cut off?"

The man passed a hand over his eyes.

"Well, sir, all this mortarin' came down, an' then the machine-guns started, an' they're all firin' at the patrol." I rounded on him. The only way to steady a man whose nerve is going is to take a firm hand with him and try to jolt him back to normal.

"You're nothing but a bloody menace, man. Get a grip on yourself. Get up and we'll go down to the patrol. There's nothing cut them off, and there's nobody firing at them. Get up."

The man got to his feet, and, still ducking spasmodically, began to follow as I picked up my rifle and moved off in the direction of the patrol.

We got about halfway. I looked every now and then over my shoulder to see that the man was still with me, then, as a fresh burst of machine-gun fire hissed and cracked above us, he grabbed my sleeve.

"Stop, sir. I can't go down there, we'll both get killed. They've killed the patrol already. They're bound to get us as well." He began to whimper.

Feeling particularly brutal, I seized the man's shoulders with both hands, and shook him till every tooth in his head rattled.

"Steady up, man, steady. For Christ's sake get a grip on yourself. There's nothing there I tell you. You'll see in a minute."

The man's whimpering had ceased, and though he was still trembling, his voice was steady enough when he answered:

"I'm sorry, sir. I'll be all right now."

For the remainder of the walk down to the patrol, I could see him taking hold of himself, and forcing himself to steadiness. We reached a point about twenty yards away from the listening post, and I coughed once or twice as we went on. Men had been shot before then by creeping up on their own patrols. I stopped a few yards short of the actual position. Carlin would be on.

"Everything all right, Carlin?" I called. Out of the darkness of the hedge came the reply.

"Oh, it's you, sir. Aye, everything's all right. What are they firin' at?"

"I don't know. I expect it's just on fixed lines though. You haven't seen anything at all?"

"Not a thing, sir."

"All right. Well, we'll get back."

We turned and made our way in silence back to the troop lines, and when we reached my trench, I turned to the other man at my side.

"Sit down a minute, I want to talk to you."

I talked to him like a father for about fifteen minutes, then sent him off, and crept into my trench. It was filled with mosquitoes, as I had forgotten to cover up the door when I went out, and the time was three minutes to four.

The next day found me sore-eyed and tired, and I made up my mind to sleep most of the day, if possible. I had

165

just made this momentous decision, when a man came along and reported to me.

"Sir. There's a bomb landed just along the hedge there and not gone off."

"How big is it?"

"I don't know, sir, but it's a hell of a deep hole."

"Well, let's have a look. It's not ticking or anything like that, is it?"

"I don't think so, sir."

We went along the line of the hedge, until we came to the hole, which was about three feet across at the top. It looked as if the bomb had gone in at a slight angle. Cautiously, I peered down into the shaft-like cavity. I never had liked explosive in any form, and had a deep rooted mistrust of anything German that was lying about.

"Do you think we should get a party an' start diggin', sir?"

"No fear. There's some chaps at Brigade who are supposed to do that sort of thing. We can send for them. And when they're here, you keep well out the road."

I went back to Troop H.Q., and made my report to Len, who got on the phone to H.Q. and gave the story to them.

"They'll send someone down from Brigade this afternoon. Anything else happen along your way last night?"

"Nothing special. There weren't any casualties down here were there?"

"No, touch wood. We've been lucky up to now in this place."

That afternoon, the sergeant from Brigade arrived to look at the unexploded bomb. I quickly decided if anyone were slap-happy it was this chap. His attitude to the whole thing was casual, too casual. He looked carelessly into the hole, nodded, and said:

"The best thing is to get a party digging, and when they get near the bomb itself, they can go fairly carefully, sir, and then I'll have a look at it."

I looked at him.

"*You* supply the men and *you* do the digging, and then

166

you can have a look at it," I said pointedly, and firmly. The sergeant looked pained.

"It's safe enough, sir," he said. "There's nothing to worry about." I almost began to enjoy myself.

"That's good," I said, "then we can come and watch you."

And so the matter was settled. The hole was roped off, the engineer sergeant went peevishly away to collect the men and the spades, and I went back to my trench to try and get some sleep.

The remainder of the day passed quietly enough, and the first half of the night was a repetition of the night before. With the dawn stand-to came a rattle of machine-gun fire, and the sound of the bullets seemed much closer than usual. As there was quite a heavy ground mist, it was quite possible that an enterprising enemy patrol had been able to get fairly close without being seen, but Len, sitting at the edge of his trench, thought it was much more likely that the patrol had got lost in the fog, and had been startled into opening up on hearing the sound of the reliefs going to the listening posts. There was no doubt, however, that the bullets were pretty close overhead. He had just made up his mind on that score, when Sergeant Jones, who was walking over to the Bren position, not ten yards away from Len's trench, was suddenly bowled clean over. He gave a yelp, grabbed his arm, and Len, peering out at him called cannily:

"Come in here and I'll fix it up."

He bandaged the wound with the field dressing placed in such a way that it acted as a tourniquet to stop the bleeding from the severed artery, and phoned the Doc.

That was the first casualty we had had in the troop for several days, but more were to follow. The following afternoon, while out on a digging party, another man was hit by splinters from a mortar, and two days afterwards two more went while on a patrol. All four had been old members of the troop, not reinforcements, which made it even worse, for the number of original members was by now at a very low level.

It was now toward the middle of August and semi-official rumours began to circulate, that the enemy in the wood opposite were about to pull out, that the big advance was about to commence on a huge front. As if to support the rumour, a message came down to the unit to the effect that a Commando guard was to be supplied immediately for Montgomery's Headquarters. A detachment from No. 4 under Len Coulson along with another detachment from No. 6 were sent off at once, and the rest of us sank back into a fresh period of waiting.

This time we did not have long to wait. On the morning of the eighteenth the allied front, for so long more or less static, burst into action. The main thrust was delivered by armoured and motorized columns which were to penetrate and encircle whole enemy divisions, in their superb sweep to the Rhine. Falaise was to become the burial-ground of an entire Germany Army, encircled by armour then shot to pieces from the air. Under the irrepressible Patton, the American armour began its phenomenal dash across France, culminating in the historic message to Eisenhower, sent by Patton as he stood by the Rhine.

On the morning of the eighteenth, however, we in No. 4 Commando had no inkling of these things as we shouldered our kit and set out along the road running through No. 3 Commando's position in order to by-pass the wood. We marched for some three hours until we reached the village of Bavent, which had apparently been evacuated only that morning by the enemy. So we plodded on as far as the neighbouring cluster of houses that was Bricqueville where we took up position and waited for the next development.

During the afternoon the Brigadier was summoned to General Gale's H.Q., where the Airborne Divisional Commander outlined his plan. It was an audacious one of infiltration, brigade by brigade, between the strong points held by the enemy. It would mean attacking by day and by night, and the brigades would move in a series of leapfrogs, so that one would march, fight and hold, the second would go through the first and repeat the operation, then the first would repeat it again.

Mills-Roberts returned to his Brigade H.Q., amidst a welter of maps and with very little time to brief his commanding officers and set the Brigade in motion. There was no time for reconnaissance. He outlined the general situation, then issued his orders quickly, so that the individual C.O.s could in turn brief their own officers, who would have time to give their men only the barest details before the Brigade set out. As far as the troops were concerned, nothing happened until the early part of the evening, when the C.O. was summoned away to the conference. The men had settled down philosophically to their last brew-up of the day. When the C.O. got back it was already about eight o'clock, and he called a troop leaders' conference immediately. He told us that there was very little time as we were to move off at dusk, we had to march quite a considerable distance, to a place called L'Epine, where we would make a dawn attack on an important crossroads which was bound to be held. During the following day, they would hold this position until one of the Parachute battalions worked its way round from the right flank and would push through to the heights of the plateau overlooking the Dives valley. The other Commandos had similar tasks. It would be an infiltration on a Brigade scale. Nothing was known about the strength of the opposition they were likely to meet, but it was thought that the enemy would be in a rather disorganized state, and that the resistance he put up was likely to be in small isolated pockets rather than as a united front.

The next point was the one of routes, and here the thing became complicated in the extreme. We were all issued with fresh maps of the new area, which, naturally was completely unfamiliar to us, time was short and we could not therefore study and memorize the details properly. The light was already beginning to go, each troop leader was concerned with his own particular troop task, and not so much with how to get to the place, which we all instinctively left to the I.O. as being his pigeon, and when we finally went to warn the troops, few of us had more than a very hazy idea of the actual road we were to follow.

At dusk we set out, and there began the march that every man who took part will remember as a sort of nightmare. The first few miles were uneventful enough, and we reached the line of railway that was to be our main axis of advance as far as the objectives, which lay some eight hundred yards to the left of the railway. The railway itself, the track and sleepers, had been removed, and only the bed of crunchy, slithering stones remained. At the side, there was a very narrow track, only inches wide, along which we tried to walk.

The night was one of Stygian darkness, and as we stumbled along the track it was impossible to see the man in front. With each momentary halt there was a succession of thuds, clanks and oaths as the procession concertina'd to a stop. If the stop was of more than a moment's duration, everyone sat down, and the inevitable result was when the column moved off again, the fact was unnoticed by someone about halfway down the line, and the unit was split into two parts, one of which was mobile, the other static. The static half would finally realize the situation, scramble to its feet, and lurch into a shambling double after the first half. The only method of finding them was by running into them, and the first few men of the hurrying latecomers would pile up on the rearmost men of the front half. Then the whole process would begin again.

At one point, we had to ford the River Dives, which was not a difficult feat for the first men, but by the time two or three whole troops had scrambled down the bank at one side, through the water, or across the duckboard bridge that had been erected, and up the bank at the other side, the slopes were so muddy and slippery that the rearmost men arrived at the top of the first bank, shot headlong down into the water, stumbled through to the far side, and then found it impossible to clamber up the smooth mud of the far bank. The resultant noise seemed enough to waken the dead, for as men grow tired, they become less and less careful in smothering their curses, hanging on to their shovels, rifles, picks and the numerous other pieces of accoutrement that can clank. Nevertheless, no fire came down on us, no sentries challenged us, and the irregular progress was maintained.

Over on the left, a gun fired continuously, the shells whining over our heads to crash somewhere on the right. From time to time a Very light would soar up into the blackness of the sky on the right, and the distant rattle of a machine-gun indicated that someone was wakeful. Still we plodded on, sweating as the rucksack straps bit into our shoulders, freezing as we lay on the side of the track in one of the innumerable halts.

As there had been no time to explain to every man exactly where we were going, and how we were going to get there, most of the troops were convinced that the whole column was lost, and the resulting depression that settled on everyone, increasing as the night went on, was such that it was difficult to arouse any sort of feeling even approaching enthusiasm. The night seemed interminable, but we finally reached the point of the railway nearest the objectives, and there we settled down to wait till about half an hour before first light, when we would move into position to put in the attack.

It was here that we discovered that we were out of touch with Brigade, and a heated altercation then followed, relayed by the people sitting in between them, between the C.O. and Peter Beckett, the Signals Officer, as to the cause of the breakdown in communication. Tempers all round were becoming frayed, and the tension was in no way eased when a signaller who had dropped his code card, surreptitiously flashed a torch to look for it. This gave the C.O. an opportunity that he was not slow to take in his anti-Signals tirade, but the score was brought level when the C.O.'s batman stood up, tripped, and with a shattering roar discharged a complete Tommy-gun magazine into the air. The silence that followed was pregnant with fury.

Fortunately, before any further calamity could occur,

Brigade came on the air, and a truce was called. Shortly afterwards, we began to move into position for the attack. The enemy positions that we were to take consisted of a bridge on the extreme left, a crossroads, a strip of road about a quarter of a mile long, with orchards on either side of it, running down from the crossroads, and at the end of that strip of road, a right-angled bend with a narrow wood at the far side of it.

"C" troop had the task of taking the bridge, "D" troop the crossroads, "E" troop was to clear the orchard at the far side of the road, "F" troop was to clear the road and take up a position at the bend, the French Troops, supported by "A" troop were to go to the right flank and clear the little wood. "B" troop was in support of everyone.

"C" and "D" troops therefore led the way then branched left to their respective objectives, while the French Troops and "A" troop disappeared round to the right. Then "E" and "F" troops, who had the most direct route, went through the middle.

As I passed the C.O. to cross the orchard to the road, it was just beginning to become light. The C.O. said:

"Everything all right, Mac? Do you know where you are?"

"I think so, sir, the road should be at the other side of this orchard."

"That's right. There's one thing you'll have to watch though. I'm out of touch with the French Troops, and they're working down towards you from the top end, at the wood, so don't go shooting them up."

I groaned inwardly. Things were quite complicated enough, without having to ascertain whether any dim forms amongst the trees were Frenchmen or not before opening fire. I wished Len was there. Len was still away doing guard to Montgomery. Wearily, I set out to cross the orchard. I was dog-tired. We reached the far hedge and moved along it till we came to a gap. There was the road, right enough, and as I peered along it, it looked wholly deserted. At the other side of it I could make out the shape of a milestone, and as the leading section turned right along the edge of the road, I nipped across the road the the milestone, to check whether it was the right road. The milestone bore the inscription: DOZULE 12Km. It was the right road. I ran over to Kit Kelly at the head of the leading section, and had just time to say:

"It's all right Kit, it's the road. Slow it down a bit from now," when out of the hedge came a scuffle followed immediately by the searing blast of a machine-gun. The range was about ten yards, and I could feel the hot bullets hissing by my head. Assuming at once it was the Frenchmen, I roared to the troop:

"Get back in the orchard!"

How nobody had been hit was just one of these mysteries or miracles that happen, but the fact remains that we all got back into the orchard without loss. I then wirelessed to H.Q. that I had come under fire and thought it was the French Troops. Then suddenly there came a burst of firing from the direction of the wood, and I realized that one French troop at least was in the wood. The people in the road must therefore be Germans. Quickly we got a Bren into position at the corner of the orchard, from which it could cover the road, or some of it, and when we saw movement in the road we opened up. This brought some success, for one figure toppled out of the hedge, fell into the road, and then crawled towards us. He turned out to be a Pole, and was wounded in the head. He said there were about twenty more in the position in the bend of the road, and this information was sent to H.Q., who ordered us to stay where we were, and the French Troops in the wood would drive the enemy out to us. So we stayed put.

Meanwhile, all round the area of the objectives, odd bursts of firing were heard. It was almost broad daylight now, and we could see clearly across the orchard. Then there came firing from the wood, the Bren stuttered in the corner, and all was going well until "E" troop, coming under fire from somewhere, opened up through their hedge and the bullets, passing over "F" troop, hissed across over "A" troop at the other side of the orchard. "A" at once retaliated with their "K" guns, and we in "F" troop found ourselves literally between two fires. To complicate matters even further, Phillippe Kieffer with the French Troops in the wood found a German mortar and ammunition, thought it would be a good idea to use it, and proceeded to plaster the orchards where "E" and "F" troops were already leading a fairly unhappy existence.

After a time, the firing died down, and there came only one further spasm, this time from the Germans in the bend of the road, and it was unfortunate that this burst hit one man in "F" troop in the head. We got him away to the R.A.P.* over by H.Q., and the stretcher party had just returned when the air was filled with the scream of shells, and a line of bursts appeared at the far side of the orchard. This was followed up by another line, this time nearer, and then still more. Some idiot at Brigade or somewhere had given the wrong code-word and brought down the barrage on the line of the enemy positions, now occupied by the unfortunate "F" troop, instead of away beyond them on the retreating enemy.

The troop was not yet dug in, so we were lying as low as possible in the shallow ditch round the field. I had never experienced fear like it. I lay in the ditch, and as each successive salvo burst nearer than the preceding one, I watched the trunk of the tree in the hedge about a foot above my head. Every burst slashed fresh scars in the bark of the trunk, and bits of wood showered down on us in the ditch, and the nearer the bursts came, the less we seemed to hear the bang, only a horrible rushing sound, and then the hot blast of the explosion.

Between the salvoes, I stuck my head up from the ditch and screamed to Burns, the signaller, who was in the only ready-made trench:

"Tell them to stop the barrage. It's our own stuff."

Burns disappeared into the trench again, another furious salvo screamed and thundered, and then he reappeared.

* Regimental Aid Post.

174

"H.Q. say there's nobody firing," he yelled, and promptly disappeared again as yet another lot arrived.

I resigned myself to despair. There was no escape this time, another two or three salvoes and the shells would be in on top of us. I was conscious of a deep-rooted hatred for the man who was firing the guns, although I knew it wasn't his fault, and then as I heard the dreaded swoosh of the next batch from the 25-pounders I closed my eyes, flattened my face in the dirt at the foot of the ditch, and waited for the death I believed to be inevitable. After the eruption had subsided, there came a pause, we realized that the miracle had happened. The barrage had stopped. When a decent interval had elapsed, I crept out from the ditch. The nearest bursts were six paces from the edge.

I went round the troop. Two men were suffering from the effects of shock and blast. They were taken to the R.A.P. and the troop began to dig in before anything else could happen. By this time numerous prisoners has been taken by the other troops, and the objectives were held by the unit.

About two hours passed, and the troop was dug in. I went round to H.Q. to see the casualties from the shelling, and on the way back, I had just come into the troop area, when I heard a sound I had not heard since D-day, but which I recognized at once with a sort of chill as Moaning Minnies. The last time they had been fire bombs. The sound was slightly right of me, and I crouched in the lee of the hedge, and bank, and waited. About twenty seconds after the first rasping warning, the bomb burst in the field with a shattering crash. Though under the bank, I was hurled into the trench occupied by one of the troop, several yards from the point where I had been standing. I dragged myself out and ran round the edge of the orchard to my own trench, leapt in, and had been there only a few seconds when we heard the next grating in the distance. Then the calamity happened.

With an explosion like the end of time, the bomb burst on one of the troop trenches, and when the blast had subsided we rushed over to the place. It had landed on the edge of the trench, so had affected the neighbouring ones as well and nine casualties resulted from the one bomb. We dug out those who had been buried, Vickery being the worst. His lungs had apparently been crushed by the blast, while Ostick, Livings and Carlin all had burst eardrums. Three more men were badly affected by the blast, and a further two were completely bomb-happy.

After they had been taken to the R.A.P., where the Doc was working overtime, I returned to the troop to take stock. No more bombs came, and I could go round and see how the remainder were. I found them shaken. The strength of the entire troop at the start of the day had been low enough, only thirty-three instead of its full sixty-three, but this business had brought it in one fell swoop down to twenty-one, less than section strength. I went back to my own trench. As the waves of reaction ebbed and flowed over me, I trembled in every limb, felt my face twitching, and even my breath came in hesitant gasps that were almost sobs. I lay in black despond, waiting for the spasm to pass and wondered how long it would be till I lost the whole lot.

In the afternoon it began to rain. As we were dug in in a ditch, the trenches all filled pretty rapidly, and night came with the twenty-one miserable members of the troop working out a sentry roster, and baling the water from our sodden trenches. The deluge continued, however, and we resigned ourselves to a night of soaking, mosquito-ridden misery.

All night I sat huddled in a gas-cape on the edge of my trench. I had recovered from the first reaction to the morning's blow. It had been nobody's fault, simply one of those unavoidable strokes of evil luck that happen. Of the casualties of the day, only two were really bad. One was Travers, who had been hit in the head, the other was Vickery. The others would all live, though I doubted whether more than half would ever be completely fit again. I worried about the remainder of the troop. If we had another attack to do, however small the part of the troop in it, we were liable to lose more. Even if we did not do any attack, but simply sat and were mortared, or counter-attacked, we were still liable to suffer further casualties. I hated to see them go. There were so few of the original troop left now, only about seven or eight, that I had lost all heart to continue. My depression increased as the water oozed through my clothes, until I sat numb and chilled waiting for the day to break.

An hour or so before the first streaks of grey appeared in the sky, the Parachute battalion passed through along the road. They were in good shape, and when they had passed through, Grace, the Bren-gunner who was also acting cook, besides doing his full share of all the normal other troop duties and patrols and turns on sentry, got busy and produced the first brew of the new day. It worked wonders, and the morale of the whole troop rose in consequence. The rain had stopped too, and when the day broke fully, it brought with it the sun, still somewhat watery, but growing in strength and warmth. We spread our kit out to dry, and went about our duties with fresh heart. The previous day was at last behind us.

I went round to H.Q. during the morning to see what was going on, and found Knyvet Carr in somewhat chastened mood already there. It turned out that Knyvet, whose troop had been in support of the unit the previous day, and had followed from the railway in daylight, had been shocked to see the muzzle of a large enemy gun protruding from the hedge by the track. The whole unit had passed within a yard of the gun, whose crew had lain in exhausted slumber or hidden round it, and it had not been noticed until Knyvet's troop arrived. The crew was taken prisoner, and the gun forgotten until after the events of the day were over. Then, consumed with curiosity, and filled with pride at his capture, Knyvet had begun to examine the weapon. Unable to read the German inscriptions, he had fiddled around with the thing until suddenly there was a fearful explosion, and a shell of no mean calibre hurtled out in the direction of Brigade H.Q., who were sitting out in the open as they assumed that the battle was over. The resultant inquiries and recriminations were the cause of Knyvet's chastenment.

Next day we moved off in the morning, and began the plodding ascent of the hill up to the plateau above the Dives valley It was a slow process, but we marched all day, and finished up in an orchard, where we turned in under the trees. The first thing we noticed was the welcome lack of mosquitoes now that we were above the swampy area of the valley, and the second thing was the Brigadier, Derek Mills-Roberts, who was in terrific form, and came round to see the whole unit. He went all round the orchard, and chatted to each group of men, and it became clear that, although our own part had been insignificant, the Brigade operation had been successful.

While we were plodding along in the rear of the huge advance, which was fanning across France, Len and his detachment were some two hundred miles ahead with Montgomery's H.Q., which moved up with leading formations, by-passing pockets of enemy as they went. The men on the guarding party had been emphatically warned of the responsibility of their task. They had been reminded that headquarters had already been attacked by small groups of Germans who, having been cut off and left by the advancing columns, still had arms and were capable of operating as raiding parties.

Len and his party, however, had gone straight from their slit-trenches to do this guard duty. They were accustomed to challenging once then firing, if no satisfactory reply were forthcoming. So aggressive were they in this business of challenging any figures in the dusk that various members of the H.Q. were almost scared to come out' of their caravans at night without first hailing the nearest sentry and informing him of their intention.

Each day they had a sort of information period, when they were given a situation report of the course of the battle. The advances made by the different columns were astounding in their audacity and speed. But all the time, away on

the left flank, the 6th Airborne Division and the 1st Special
Service Brigade struggled along on foot, carrying on what
seemed to us to be a private little war of our own.

We passed through the burning ruins of Pont L'Eveque
to embark upon another Brigade infiltration between
enemy strong points to take up positions behind them.
Again it was an operation which had been hastily planned,
to meet the demands of the moment. In the troops of the
unit we knew very little of the routes, and simply marched
along behind the leaders, running when they ran, stopping
when they stopped. At one stage the unit was split in two
when we made a detour through a wood.

Behind me was Phillippe Kieffer, intrepid as ever,
driven forward through the darkness by a mixture of
natural determination, intense hatred of the Germans, and
from time to time a judicious swig at his flask.

When a man came panting up from somewhere in the
rear to gasp out the news that half the unit had gone astray
in the wood, I heard Phillippe say in stricken tones:

"O my Gawd." There followed the sound of a stopper
being drawn, a long gurgling sound, a gusty sigh, then he
tapped me on the shoulder as we strode on without having
slackened speed:

"'Ave you 'eard? 'Alf the 'ole unit is missing. *Mon Dieu,
quelle nuit.*"

I had little time to answer, however, for at this stage
No. 3 Commando, who had been in the lead, bore off from
our line of advance, and we continued on our own. Most
of the missing troops had somehow caught up with us again,
and when we came to a halt in a leafy lane, we fell asleep
where we sat. This bliss did not last long, however. I
happened to be nearest the C.O. as he groped around, map
in hand, so I was at once kicked into wakefulness.

"Get up and take a patrol and find the main road."

I was startled.

"Who me? Well, where the hell are we?"

A map was thrust into my unwilling hand. Our supposed
position was indicated by a finger making a vague move-

179

ment, which covered about fifteen miles, and I was told to get a move on.

By now the mists of the morning were rising all around us and, as we skirted a farm which loomed up ahead of us, every dog in the place seemed to be awake. We crossed an orchard and suddenly heard transport. The road seemed to be behind the far hedge, and as we approached it, another vehicle roared along it towards us. We lay in the hedge waiting to see if the car was ours or theirs. Then in the early morning light I could see on the front of a vehicle, two figures in field-grey. McVeigh saw them too and his finger curled round the trigger, when I noticed just in time that the two Germans were sitting on the bonnet of a jeep and were obviously prisoners.

A few minutes later the Commando marched to its destination, a group of farm buildings, where we stayed for the rest of that day. The last of the Germans in the district had apparently pulled out about an hour before we arrived there, and at first the inhabitants had thought we were another detachment withdrawing, as there had been various convoys and columns moving through most of the previous day and night.

It was by now fairly obvious to us all that the war was moving much too fast for us to keep up with it for long. Next day we marched in brilliant sunshine through the town of Beuzeville, where the people crowded out into the streets, cheering and waving, and thrusting bottles into the ready hands of the marching men. Most of these folk were genuinely delighted to see us, particularly the older generation, many of whom stood, with tears of joy coursing down furrowed cheeks, saluting as we passed. They were saluting not us as men, but the return of their self-respect.

In a side-street a slatternly-looking young woman was screaming and struggling as a group of men with tricolour armbands sheared and shaved the hair off her head. Two or three other young women, already shorn, stood weeping by the roadside, as they helped one another to wrap a scarf or a kerchief around their baldness. They looked repulsively sexless with their white domes above the heightened colour of their faces.

About three miles beyond the town we marched along dusty lanes, the hedges of which were already full of ripe hazel-nuts. On either side were orchards in which rosy apples hung heavy on the trees. Here we halted. Each troop was given an area, an orchard with a barn filled with sweet-smelling straw. It was just like heaven. The date was 26 August.

For the first three days we slept for about fifteen hours of the twenty-four. Most of the waking hours were spent lying in the sun, stretching out a lazy hand for another apple, soaking in the warmth of the sun which shone steadily down from a cloudless sky.

Up to the time we reached this haven, we had been in action continuously over a period of eighty-two days and eighty-two long nights, in which time we had not once been relieved. Our casualties in this stretch were more than one hundred per cent of our original strength, for as fast as replacements had arrived, they were hit. In "F" troop we still had about nine of the original sixty-three.

As we lay basking in the sunshine in our Elysian orchards, the war for us was very remote, but for the French troops it was as real as ever. Most of them were frantic for news of their homes and families, which were being liberated daily, as the tide of battle swept past them. The news of the liberation of Paris sent a surge of joy through them all. Several of them obtained leave to go there and find their relations.

Guy Vourch and Phillippe Kieffer arrived in Paris together. The town was still wild with excitement. They separated and Guy hurried to the rue Faubourg St. Honoré where Brigitte had stayed. He was in a turmoil of excitement. Yet when he arrived and saw her standing before him, the words he had prepared died, and though his whole being sang he became inarticulate and formal.

It did not surprise him to find his mother and two sisters already there. They had been forced to leave Finisterre hurriedly and go into hiding in Paris. With them he felt more at ease, and after the initial surprise at seeing him thus, suddenly after three and a half years, they on their side gave him all the news of his father and brothers. Of these, one brother, having gone with the Leclerc Division all the way from Lake Chad to Libya, and thence via Tunisia on the long road to France, had finally been killed just outside Paris only a few days before.

His father, after a fairly hectic time in the early days, when he had spent his time between spying on German shipping at Brest and relaying the information to the British, and helping to run "Johnny" escape route, had been taken by the Germans, then by some blunder released, whereupon he escaped to North Africa, where he was when the Allies landed. The last they had heard from him, he had made his way to England, where presumably he still was.

The day passed quickly, as the strangeness wore off, and Guy in his turn, gave the story of his own adventures since he had last seen them. They listened with interest, and he was conscious of a sense of warmth, a feeling of homecoming, and the feeling of pride as they all sat there. They had all of them done their utmost throughout the period of France's humiliation to keep alive a tradition. Each one in his or her own way had taken the hard road, when so many of their compatriots had followed the easy one. There had been times when their efforts had seemed futile in the face of the vast occupying organization, when their obstinate refusal to recognize the German authority had seemed almost a childish unwillingness to face facts. But now all that was gone. They had outlived the occupation, and although one brother was gone, they were proud that he had died making his effort to free France, their France, from the serfdom to which it had been condemned.

Next day Guy had to return to the unit. He left his family light-heartedly enough, feeling as though he were years younger. A great weight had been lifted from his mind. He realized for the first time how heavy had been the load of worry which he had for so long carried with him. Now at last he was able to think of the future in terms of home and family, without wondering if indeed there would be such a thing. To Brigitte he had said nothing of any importance. In her presence he still felt a certain reserve, although the first stammering confusion had passed.

He met Phillippe. To him the journey to Paris had brought tragic news. His son, whom he had left almost a schoolboy still, had been killed a bare two days previously, fighting for the *Maquis*. Phillippe, who had worshipped the boy, crumpled under the blow. He had come so near to being re-united. Now his world had crashed about his ears. The eagerness with which he had hastened to Paris had given way to an apathy normally quite foreign to his vigorous nature. In silence they made the journey back.

After three more days of sleeping and basking in the sunshine, rumours began to circulate about a return to Blighty. Fearing that such a move would take place while Len Coulson was still away, and not daring to reach England without him, as I would have to explain to Jill Coulson the reason for his absence, I wrote a note to Len, telling him the position, and sent a despatch-rider off into the blue to find Montgomery's H.Q. and give Len the message. I had, of course, no authority to do this, but reckoned that if Len got back in time, everything would be all right, and with all the coming and going around the unit in the meantime, the D.R. would never be missed.

A few of us visited Deauville, which was still in a pretty battered state. We made our way into a little bar, where the proprietor, after making us welcome and regaling us with stories of the indescribably disorganized flight of the German forces in the area, looked round in a conspiratorial manner and asked us whether we would like some champagne, but of the best, which he himself had kept hidden from the *sales Boches* throughout the occupation. It was only because we were, in a sense the liberators of his country, and had stood by de Gaulle, that he was prepared to let us have even two bottles of this nectar. He named a price which brought me out in a cold sweat of fright. No champagne on earth was worth that much. Still, we had spent no money whatsoever during the last three months. We signified our approval of his suggestion.

With due ceremony the bottles were set upon the table. The wads of notes were paid over. The proprietor, having put the glasses down in front of us, opened one bottle, bowed to us all and disappeared. The wine was pleasant enough. We opened the other bottle, and I caught the cork as it popped.

"How's that?" Denny Rewcastle called, and I opened my hand and showed him the cork. Then: "Hallo, what's that mark on the cork?"

I looked down. The cork bore the stamp of the German eagle and swastika.

On the morning of 6 September, we were warned to move, and in the early afternoon the Commando marched out from its orchards on to the main road where we then sat down to await the transport which was to take us down to Arromanches. There was still no sign of Len Coulson and his party, and I was becoming worried at his non-appearance. A huge convoy of American vehicles carrying petrol to the columns a long way ahead passed along. From each cab there came a flash of white teeth and the wave of a dusky hand. When the dust settled another convoy came round the bend the other way. This was a smaller group of vehicles. They drew to a halt when they reached us. It was Len Coulson and his guard.

Half an hour later we set off back towards the coast, and the next morning we marched on board the *Ulster Monarch* at the Mulberry harbour.

On our arrival in England we were sent first of all to a camp at Petworth. We reached there late in the evening, but were delighted to find a number of our own troop there to welcome us. These were the early casualties, who were not fit enough to rejoin us. The situation called for a reunion party, so Len and I went to the nearest bank, armed with the cheque-book for the troop fund. We drew a cheque and returned to camp to collect the troop and arrange for transport into Guildford.

That evening we thronged into a quiet pub in Guildford, laid fifteen pounds on the counter before the astonished eyes of the manageress and gave the order: "Just keep it coming, Ma."

It was a great night. There was a piano in the corner, we dragged in a passing pianist, as the troop performers were busy, and settled down. We drank to the living, we drank to the dead, we drank to the past, the present, the future.

Next day we went on leave for fourteen whole days.

CHAPTER VII

Red on the darkness the streamers run,
Of a flame that is not of the rising sun.
OGILVIE: *Whaup o' the Rede*

FOR the first time since I had joined the Commando, I found the leave too short. Every time I sat down in a chair I fell asleep. I went to the pictures and slept through two feature films, but the screaming of a shell in the news-reel of the battle-fronts had me under the seat before I realized where I was. I longed for the company of the others, yet I dreaded what it might involve. I felt I wanted to lie watching the snails rushing past, but I was restless and somehow ill at ease.

On our return to Petworth, we were told that we would probably be sent to the Far East in a short time. We attended lectures on jungle warfare, where we were told the differences between the war as we had known it and the war as we would soon come to know it.

Then suddenly came the movement order, not to the Far East, but back to France. No. 4 was to be detached from the First Special Service Brigade, the remainder of which was to stay for the meantime in England, and we were to become a part of the Fourth Special Service Brigade. Here we would be the only Army Commando unit in the Brigade, the others all being Royal Marine.

This news was not particularly well received. The Army Commando units were all volunteer units. They had been the founders of the whole Commando business, and at the start it had been a very difficult task to get into a Commando. Most of the men, and the officers too, had given up rank and in most cases the possibility of promotion, in order to serve in a Commando, and it was not until the field army closed its ranks to us, that the majority of the Royal Marine

Commandos were formed, although there had been two volunteer R.M. Commandos which had served from the early days. At any rate, whatever the cause, there was a certain amount of feeling between the Army Commandos and the Royal Marines, many of whom felt that they, with their long-established tradition, should have supplied the early raiding forces, instead of being drafted into new formations, sent to Achnacarry to go through a rigorous training, then to be issued with a green beret.

We had liked being with our old friends in No. 3 and No. 6 Commandos, and we were sorry to leave them, but on 6 October we crossed from Newhaven to Dieppe and moved from there into Belgium. Near Ostende, in a little place called den Haan, we moved into billets and began training.

As I looked round the troop on our first parade in our new surroundings, every second face seemed to be new. Training would have to be by sub-sections, so that the new members would grow accustomed to working with the others. We were lucky in having so many of our wounded back again, and these along with the redoubtable McVeigh, now a sergeant, Percy Toombs, ex-Grenadier and one of the original members of the troop. Taff Edwards as C.S.M., and others of the same calibre, would form the backbone of the new troop.

We had as yet no idea of our next task. The fact that we had been so hastily brought back indicated that something was afoot, but so far our orders had been merely to get fit. So, to start with, we played football every day, did one cross-country run per week, and carried out innumerable field-firing exercises in the dunes between den Haan and Ostende. This training could be quite realistic as there were very strong enemy defence works in the area. So, under cover of smoke and H.E. from the mortars, we put in attacks on pill-boxes, gun-pits and emplacements.

The war by this time had pushed on well into Belgium and indeed as far as the German frontiers on the other fronts. The enemy were holding out in pockets around the estuary of the Scheldt and still controlled the greater part of

Holland. After the failure at Arnhem, where success would almost certainly have shortened the war by months, there seemed every prospect of a long and dreary winter campaign. About the third week of October, the first inkling of our task reached us. It seemed that we were to be given a direct assault on some heavily defended area, as yet unnamed. Troop leaders were warned that street-fighting would almost certainly be necessary, and were told to prepare their troops accordingly. An area in the outskirts of Ostende was set aside for us. We went there troop by troop, to spend days clambering up and down walls, moving through rows of houses, using smoke-grenades to cross open squares, using toggle-ropes to scale the walls of houses. I was always amazed at the ease with which some of the troop could climb walls. Old Donkin and McVeigh for example, both of whom loathed marching, were as nimble as cats in nipping up the side of a house.

During the last week of October the C.O. summoned the troop commanders and told them that the objective was to be Flushing, the port on the island of Walcheren. The Germans had spent four years in fortifying the place, but the R.A.F. had breached the main sea-dykes on the island in two places, one just outside Flushing, one at the other side of the island. The main part of the island was now under water, although only the outskirts of Flushing were affected.

A governing feature in any assault on the town was its physical shape. Flushing falls very sharply into two parts, the old dock area and the new, rather more residential area. These two parts are separated by a neck of land about four hundred yards wide, upon which are two main road junctions connecting the old and the new parts of the town. If therefore the Commando could land, push straight through the old part of the town to seize these two road junctions, hold them, and clear the old part up to them, the follow-up troops could then push through into the new part and clear that.

The difficulty lay in getting ashore. The sea-wall seemed

in itself a complete obstacle to any seaborne assault, while every possible landing area was exposed to a system of mutually supporting strongpoints and pill-boxes.

That evening our thoughts were rather gloomy. We knew from experience that things seldom turn out as bad as they at first look, but the odds were in this case so heavily in favour of the defenders that it seemed inevitable that we would have heavy casualties. Our only chance would be to land in darkness, and try to rush the initial obstacles.

Over a glass of singularly unpleasant Belgian beer Len Coulson and I talked of anything but the coming action. We were both depressed. "The trouble with this Commando business," said Len, "is that you get to know the blokes too well."

"I know," I said, "and it gets worse the longer you go on." We thought of the friends we had already lost.

Len thrust his glass away. "Filthy stuff," he said. "Let's try the cognac." We did so.

Next day we were allocated troop tasks in the plan for the assault. Everything hinged on the initial landing. The Commando plan was simple, the tasks of each troop were clear. If the landing were successful, there was a reasonable chance that the whole Commando could be ashore and striking towards their objectives before the garrison, which would be under a colossal bombardment, had realized that a landing in any strength had been made.

On the last day of October, we moved up to Breskens, which was to be our jumping-off point. It had been battered unmercifully in the recent fighting, so that it now scarcely resembled a town at all. In the little harbour, which was almost unserviceable, lay the landing-craft, and that afternoon we carried out a practice embarkation under cover of a smoke screen against the prying eyes which might be watching from Flushing, which was clearly visible across the water. Unfortunately, this screen lifted at the wrong moment, and as we marched away from the harbour it came under fairly heavy shellfire which added a little to the already considerable damage in that area.

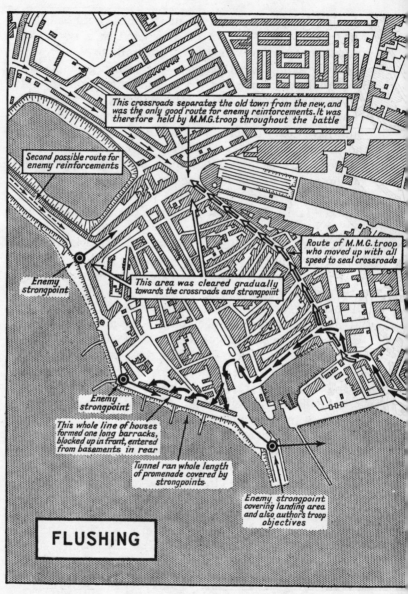

This crossroads separates the old town from the new, and was the only good route for enemy reinforcements. It was therefore held by M.M.G. troop throughout the battle

Second possible route for enemy reinforcements

Route of M.M.G. troop who moved up with all speed to seal crossroads

Enemy strongpoint

This area was cleared gradually towards the crossroads and strongpoint

Enemy strongpoint

This whole line of houses formed one long barracks, blocked up in front, entered from basements in rear

Tunnel ran whole length of promenade covered by strongpoints

Enemy strongpoint covering landing area and also author's troop objectives

FLUSHING

1 November, 1944. The amphibious assault

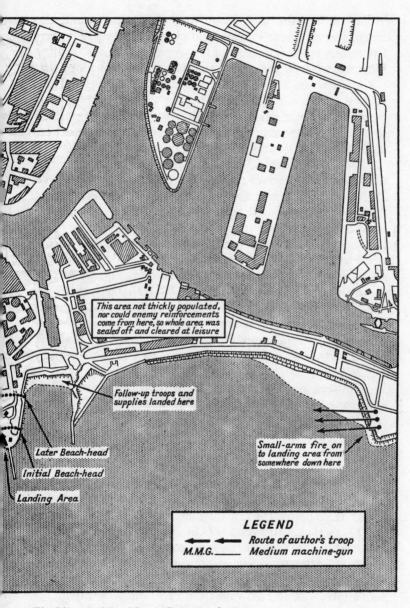

This area not thickly populated,
nor could enemy reinforcements
come from here, so whole area was
sealed off and cleared at leisure

Follow-up troops and
supplies landed here

Small-arms fire on
to landing area from
somewhere down here

Later Beach-head

Initial Beach-head

Landing Area

LEGEND
Route of author's troop
M.M.G. _____ Medium machine-gun

on Flushing, led by No. 4 Commando

In the evening before turning in, I went round the troop, just as a batch of mail caught up with us. The first two letters I gave out were for Guardsman Toombs, wishing him many happy returns of the day—reminding him that his birthday was November the first, the day of the assault. As always, I was amazed at the apparent composure of the members of the troop. They might have been on an exercise for all the excitement they showed. I was glad that the new men had settled down well with the others.

Back in the shell of the house which was our billet, we tried to make ourselves comfortable for an hour or two. We all felt the usual taut feeling, and most of us felt a little depressed. Enemy shelling of the area immediately behind Breskens did not help to make us any happier either. Only the sight of Bill Boucher-Myers, the second-in-command, who was suffering from acute indigestion, and sat morosely eating aspirins helped to cheer the rest of us, and we turned to our tins of self-heating soup in the hope that a warm drink would induce sleep. Mine was the only tin whose self-heating apparatus refused to function, and I found the cold thickish liquid quite revolting. Determinedly, we huddled in our blankets on the floor, and after a time fell into an uneasy sleep.

We were roused at a quarter to three in the morning, and groped into our equipment. The first news was that the bombing had been cancelled, owing to bad flying conditions. This led to some fervent abusing of the R.A.F., which put us all in a better frame of mind, and we marched down to the harbour to begin embarkation. As each troop had to wait its turn to use the limited space left sufficiently undamaged, it was an hour before we were all aboard.

At 04.40 hours, the leading craft, with Denny Rewcastle and his section, slipped out of the harbour. Theirs was the unenviable task of finding a landing-place and establishing a foothold. Denny, who when the opportunity arose, tended to be the long-haired silk-scarf type, never failed to do a man's job in action. At one time in France, Denny and I had been the only two unwounded subalterns remaining in the unit. He had patrolled unceasingly, without shirking or sparing himself, and had proved himself in action to be both capable and courageous.

Now he was embarking on perhaps his most unpleasant assignment. No landing-place had been fixed, although an area had been chosen as possible. It was up to Denny to seek out this area, find out whether a landing was indeed possible there, and if so land with his party, clear the area immediately around the landing-point, hang on there, establishing a little bridgehead, and signal the rest of us in.

On his judgment and on his decision hinged the success or failure of the whole operation. Whether he would remain alive to see the result was a matter of doubt.

Five minutes after their departure, the barrage started, as the remaining craft were just clearing the end of the harbour entrance. The din was immense. Soon we could see fires breaking out in the town across the water. We cruised around in the river, listening to the screaming of the shells overhead and to the crashing reverberations of the explosions, feeling all the while the drizzling rain falling like mist upon us, while Rewcastle's party was working its way inshore towards a mole which, jutting out from the sea-wall seemed the likeliest place for a landing area.

Inside the landing-craft, quietly chugging in a wide circle, we kept our eyes turned anxiously towards the darkness of the shoreline. The flashes of the bursts and the red glare of the fires in the background seemed to exaggerate the inky blackness at the level of the water. McVeigh stirred beside me. "Wonder 'ow they're gettin' on," he said. His black-streaked face looked curiously shapeless in the reddish glow from the shore, only the gleam of his black eyes could not be camouflaged. Restlessly he shifted round in his seat. His gaze fell on a sailor. "Why don't you bloody matloes ever clean these things out?" he growled. "There's oil all over the place."

Just where the wooden pier joined the mole proper, the landing-party touched down. They scrambled ashore, slipped and stumbled on the wet stonework of the dykes, and groped their way forward as far as the line of stakes on the side of the mole. The crashing of the explosions on the town was deafening, there was no need to speak in whispers, at times it was all they could do to hear a word of command. Looking upward to the town they could see against the flames the outline of a windmill, its gaunt arms raised despairingly. The leading man forced two of the stakes a little way apart and slipped through. Behind him came one who had a roll of white tape attached to his belt. The tape unrolled as he moved forward, marking for those following the track known to be safe. Purposefully, the little group moved up towards the pill-boxes on the mole.

Out in the river, we lay in our craft and saw the light winking towards us from the darkness below the glare of the burning town. We stopped our circling and made for the shore.

When we were still about three hundred yards offshore, some 20-millimetre cannon opened up somewhere on the left. The red streaks of tracer swooshed and cracked a few feet over the craft. We felt like Aunt Sally at the fair, with our heads sticking up above the sides of the L.C.A. as we peered at the outline of the landing-ground drawing nearer. Machine-guns joined in with the cannon-fire from the left, but they too were firing high. An L.C.A. is more or less invisible from the shore at night, the only sign of its presence being the white of the water where the blunt bows thrust their way forward. The gunners on shore were doubtless aiming about normal deck level, hoping to cause casualties among the naval personnel handling the craft, but as we were low in the water, the streams of fire were passing for the most part overhead.

In the last stages of the run-in the fire was fairly heavy, those on shore having by now realized that our barrage had indeed lifted, and that we were on our way in. They finally succeeded in sinking two L.C.A.s a few yards from the shore and causing some casualties amongst the crew.

Scrambling ashore on to the slimy stonework of the mole along with McVeigh, who was always glad to get out of any sort of boat, we saw the tape, followed it through the stakes and heard the cheerful voice of Lieutenant Harry Hargreaves, the Navy signaller and demolition king, calling out as we all swarmed up the dyke towards him: "Mind the light, chaps, mind the light. You can't beat the old firm, can you?" Harry had been with No. 4 before at Lofoten and Dieppe.

The time was now 06.30 hours and the beachhead was established. Speed was now essential, as the initiative lay with us. We met no opposition as we hurried along in the half-light, although it was eerie to see dim figures flitting across the streets and not to know whether they were Dutch civilians taking refuge, or Germans.

As we ran on, threading our way through the dim streets, every man was probably going over in his mind the details of the route as we had all memorized it from the aerial photographs. In the lead was Peter Mercer-Wilson's old section under its new leader Nick Barrass, a tall, quiet-spoken policeman, who had played football for Gateshead. He had come to us at a difficult time, just before the big advance through France had started, so it was not until the training for this Flushing operation that we had really got to know him. Now as he and his section hurried towards our objectives, a terrific crash from time to time denoted an odd "short" from the artillery, while chunks of house frequently toppled down simply as a result of the vibration of the explosions.

In the briefing for the job, we had agreed that we would under no circumstance engage any enemy on the way through the town, unless they were directly between us and our objectives. So when we suddenly came under burst after burst of machine-gun fire from the left, which dropped two men in their tracks, we broke sharply to the right into the cover of houses and shops, so that we could work our way towards the objectives from the landward side.

I glanced at my watch. Only some ten minutes had elapsed since we left the landing area. Nick's objective now lay to our left front, while mine, a line of barracks, was to the right. My section branched off without a pause, and as we passed, Nick raised his arm in a wave.

"Good luck, Mac," he said. I waved back as I ran past. Nick and his men forced an entry into their block of buildings and began to clear them, working their way quickly from room to room upwards. Near the top was a spiral staircase, Nick and Sergeant Fraser were making their way up, covering each other's advance as far as possible. They were about two-thirds of the way up, with Fraser in the lead and Nick covering him from the bend in the stair below him. He was crouching there, below the level of a little window and was unable to see the sniper in the floor above in the house opposite. The range was not very great and Nick was killed instantly.

Meantime we were heading for our barracks on the seafront, with McVeigh like a bristling terrier in the lead. We dashed down an alleyway, at the foot of which we found a row of little houses. Beyond these was the back of what appeared to be a garage, which was very close to the barracks. There was a hole in the back wall of this garage, which McVeigh quickly enlarged. One by one the leading group swung into the darkness of the building itself.

The other walls were wooden and flimsy, as was the door which hung ajar. The leading man reached the door and almost ran into a body of German soldiers beside the blank wall of a bunker. The Germans immediately opened fire into and through the walls of the garage. I was just coming through the hole at the back, saw the disadvantage and roared: "Back out this way."

Then it was that old Donkin, who at forty-one was the oldest member of the Commando, ex-miner, old soldier, the father of nine children, with a tenth on the way, jumped into the doorway and stood there framed, with both feet planted firm, stocky body balanced on slightly bandy legs, and methodically started to Tommy-gun from left to right among the fifteen or so Germans visible to him by the concrete bunker. He reached the right-hand end of his swing and was starting the return, when one man on the left, whom he had missed at the start, got in a quick shot. It took him straight through the throat, killing him at once. McVeigh, who was beside him with a rifle, made no mistake with his return shot, then doubled back through the now empty garage, through the gap in the wall, and out to us in the alleyway.

The tempo now became even quicker. The enemy knew exactly where we were, and if organized could bring fire down on us from the various vantage points amongst the buildings around us. We could not afford to lose the initiative.

Between us and the barracks stood a number of sheds and outhouses. We scrambled up on to the wall, and with Sergeant Miles in the lead, dashed across the splintered and rotten tiles of the shed roofs. Twice I went through the tiles on the way across, to stick sweating and struggling between the rafters, before finally reaching the lane at the other side.

From this lane we burst into the barracks at basement level, and while Sergeant Miles and his section held and explored the basement, McVeigh's men rushed upwards through the building clearing every room. I tagged along with McVeigh. Each room was dealt with in the same way. As one man kicked the door in and leapt to the far side of the room, his partner stood obliquely across the passage and covered the doorway. Prisoners were sent to Sergeant Miles.

We paused on the third floor, while McVeigh wiped the sweat from his brow. "I don' like this place," he hissed.

"I don't think hellish much of it either," I answered, "but we'd better finish it off, then we can get organized." McVeigh grunted and moved slowly down the passage, which curved sharply to the left. He pressed close to the left-hand wall, while I crouched close to the wall on my right, covering his advance as well as possible.

As he drew near to the bend, he paused. From outside he could still hear the sounds of the battle in the city and the now more distant explosions of the barrage. From other parts of the building he could hear his friends as they burst open doors, the sudden shouts, the occasional shots. Then with a prickling all up and down his spine he heard something else—a stealthy slithering sound from the passage-way beyond him. He stood for a moment petrified, the sound seemed so close. Then before his horrified gaze as he pressed against the wall a bayonet point appeared. He held his breath. The bayonet inched forward as the German shuffled closer. McVeigh realized that for a right-handed man coming along the passage the other way the rifle would be next the wall and impossible to manoeuvre without the man jumping out into the middle of the passage.

Silently he sank on one knee, his own rifle drawn back for the lunge. That would also give me a possible shot if the German did jump to the side.

Inch by inch, more of the enemy bayonet appeared, then for a moment it seemed to hesitate and with a growl McVeigh smashed his own weapon upon the other, forcing it away from the wall and sprang forward, firing as he lunged, while I rushed across from my position at the other side of the passage.

The sound of the shot reverberated in the enclosed space, and with our ears still ringing, we gazed down at the man on the floor.

"I said I didn't like the bloody place," said McVeigh. "It fair gives me the creeps," and he drew his hand across his glistening brow.

We finished the remaining rooms in our part of the building and returned to Sergeant Miles, who had discovered that there was a tunnel extending the whole length of the sea-front. This tunnel had numerous openings on to the promenade itself, which was covered for its entire length by a machine-gun position on the right. As the front of the houses had been blocked to make one solid front, it was impossible for us to come out to the seaward side without presenting a sitting target to the machine-gunner. It was also possible for an enemy to come along the seaward side without our knowing, slip in behind us and cut our small band off from the rest. That meant we would have to drop one man at each of the openings as we went along. This we did for some time, but it was a slow and wearing process. I grabbed the oldest and greyest of the prisoners and told him to go and tell his friends to surrender. After a certain amount of demur, he rather reluctantly agreed. McVeigh, who had been standing impatiently by, then broke in.

"Wot's goin' on, sir? Wot's 'e say?"

"He says he's going to tell them to pack in."

"Good. I'll see 'e does an' all."

And before anyone could say anything further, the aggressive McVeigh had rammed his rifle into the man's back and was urging him along towards the doorway of the next house. They disappeared. Minutes dragged by. I began to get worried. They might quite well have hit McVeigh over the head in some dark corner, and the prisoner would then be free to tell them that there were only about eight men outside. I wished we hadn't had to drop the others off at the tunnel entries.

Just as I was beginning to despair, McVeigh appeared again, some fifty yards farther along and yelled: "'Ere they come, sir!" and a line of shambling figures stumbled out of the houses. Seventy-five men lurched past, hands clasped on head, with a triumphant McVeigh bringing up the rear.

This brought us to within fifty yards of the end of the barracks, so when we next came under fire, I got the eight men into a stable in the basement of the building. From the floor above there was a good field of fire for the Bren. We settled in and sent a message back to report on the situation.

It turned out that 5 troop, who were supposed to be in support of us, had become involved in a battle of their own and were unable to come through. We were therefore ordered to consolidate on our present position. Elsewhere the battle was apparently going just as well as it was in our case. All the first objectives had been reached on schedule, and although fighting was sharp, we still had the advantage.

In our stable in the basement, we organized ourselves for defence. The Bren had a good field of fire to the rear of the barracks, but the other side was a problem. At the end of the barracks, still some fifty yards away, the machine-gun position was still active, and we were unable to get at it. Nor could we keep an effective watch on it, as we had no access to the front, except where shell-fire had made holes in the outer wall of the houses. There was one such hole in our house, just at ground level. I discussed it with McVeigh.

"If we were in the machine-gun position and they were in here, what would you do?"

Black eyes looked up from under craggy brows. "I'd get someone along and shake them up with grenades."

"That's what they'll do too."

McVeigh nodded. "An' the folk next door'll tell 'em where we are." Between us we worked out a plan.

The hole in the wall gave on to a fair-sized room, which had a door leading on to a little landing, which in turn had doors leading off to other rooms. The door on to the landing had a panel broken. We decided to leave the front room empty, shut the door, and have Sergeant Sutherland sitting on a chair on the landing with a Tommy-gun, watching the hole in the outer wall through the hole in the panel of the landing door. Leaving him there, we then went off below, where we noisily set about the placing of the bales of straw as a barricade.

Sitting silently above us, Sutherland kept his eyes fixed on the hole in the front wall. He did not have long to wait. A pair of jackboots slipped quickly past the hole, then after a moment came back. Another pause while the German doubtless examined all that he could see of the empty room from a safe angle, then probably rejoicing at the stupidity of the attackers, he stooped and began to slide down into the room. At this point Sutherland thought the thing had gone far enough and let him have practically a whole tommy mag, which slung him straight back through the hole. We rushed up from below, and McVeigh viewed the scene with satisfaction.

"Well done, 'aggis," he said, "'e's quite 'andy there, too. If anyone else wants to get in, they'll 'ave to shift 'im first."

We returned below, where we found the others settling down to a brew, apart from the look-outs. Toombs was sitting on a bale of straw phlegmatically cleaning his rifle. I stopped in front of him. "Happy birthday, Toombs?" I asked. "Gor," he said, "I'd forgotten about that." He pondered a moment. Then he grinned. "The best bit was seeing you stuck in that roof."

As far as we were concerned, the rest of the day passed by without much excitement, but in other parts of the town, particularly in the neighbourhood of the two road junctions, fighting was more or less continuous all day, with our machine-gun sections hanging on against driving counter-attacks as the enemy tried to come to the aid of those penned in the old part of the town.

In the late afternoon Alastair Thorburn with 1 troop came from the landing area, where they had established the beachhead, through our positions and began to push on towards the strongpoint beyond the end of the barracks. As darkness fell, we decided to wait till next morning. The follow-up troops were now ashore in strength, and were due to make their thrust the next day into the new part of the town and to the batteries on the outskirts.

Next morning, the strongpoint still held out stubbornly. It was well-sited against ground attack. But we had in support the first aerial cab-rank service of the war—rocket-firing Typhoons circling overhead—and within minutes of being called, these swooped down on the enemy position in a series of terrifying attacks. We lay back and watched. After a very short time a white flag appeared, then three very shaken officers and fifty-four equally shaken men came out and gave themselves up.

Away on the other flank, Jack Wilson with 2 troop had cleared the whole of the far end of the town, which was a sort of peninsula of docks and harbour installations, so that the whole of the old part of the town was now completely cleared of the enemy.

In the landing area Harry Hargreaves had been busy blowing up the beach obstacles and clearing the whole area of mines and booby-traps. From the mole on which we landed he took out hundreds of mines which had been placed between the stakes and amongst the stonework. Had the leading man groped his way up the dyke a foot or so to either side, he would have been killed. Pure chance—luck—the hand of God—what you will, had brought him safely through, and the entire unit had followed in his footsteps.

Next day we left Flushing, crossed the breach in the dyke and worked our way along the dunes to Zoutland, where we stayed the night before going on to Domburg the following day. There was no enemy resistance on the island by this time except in the extreme north, and we were told we would push through 41 Marine Commando towards the last place in enemy hands, Vrouwenpolder.

This meant a night march along the dunes, so that we could be in a position to attack in the morning, and for once, the march was uneventful. We reached the point short of the nearest known enemy positions, and waited for dawn.

The dry land at this point was about six hundred yards wide, from the edge of the water of the sea to the edge of the water all over the island. To the seaward side there were the dunes, then came a flat strip of grassland with a single line of railway along the middle, then there was a belt of woodland, and beyond that was nothing but water.

The plan was that one French troop should be on the left, clearing the dunes of any odd positions they might contain, the other French troop and 2 troop should be on the right, clearing the woods, while the main body of the Commando, with our troop in the lead, should walk along the middle until something happened. What was to happen then, nobody quite knew, but we moved off in that formation just as dawn broke.

Going along the middle, I felt extremely conspicuous, and looked apprehensively at the outlines of the dunes on the one side, and the woods on the other, but for the first half-hour nothing at all happened. Then suddenly, from the dunes there came the rattle of a machine-gun, which seemed to be firing well behind the leading troops. In point of fact, it was firing on Commando H.Q., who quickly headed for cover in the edge of the wood. There were no casualties caused by the firing, and the advance continued.

When we drew level with the end of the wood, my party found there was a track running along by a hedge, and followed it to its end, about a hundred yards farther on. Before us was a completely open space, without a vestige of cover of any sort, and at the other side, some two hundred yards away, were several barrack-like buildings, and as we stopped at the end of the hedge, we saw a number of grey-clad figures disappear away on the right behind some farm buildings. At the barrack-like buildings there was an ominous lack of movement, and I didn't like the look of things at all. Bill Boucher-Myers came bustling up.

"There's your section objective, Mac, these buildings."

I suppose I looked doubtful; I certainly felt it.

"It's a bit open, isn't it?" I said.

"That's all right," said the second-in-command cheerfully. "We'll give you bags of support from here with the two-inch mortar."

I looked at Royle leering at me from behind the two-inch mortar, and felt no reassurance at all, but there seemed no alternative, and so I called Sergeant McVeigh and Sergeant Miles and told them the position.

"Well," said McVeigh, "'ow are we gonna do it?"

Mine is not a subtle nature.

"We'll walk across in a line till something happens," I said. "You take your sub-section on the left, and Sergeant Miles, you take yours on the right. Stick the Brens right on the flanks." I looked at the silently menacing buildings. "I suppose we'd better fix bayonets too."

So we fixed bayonets, extended into line and began to walk, with rifles at the "high port," across the open, eighteen good men and true. Nothing happened.

We got halfway across, my morale sinking lower with each step. I was convinced that the hordes of enemy in the huts were simply waiting to mow us down from close range. I decided we'd better do something, so called to the riflemen to fire a couple of rounds each from the hip. There was no reply to the ragged volley. My spirits sank even lower. They were just over fifty yards away now.

"Tell the Brens to give a good burst."

The Brens stuttered from the flanks, and still there came no answering hail of bullets from the buildings. Then suddenly a white flag appeared.

My relief knew no bounds. I had visions of hordes of Germans all wanting to surrender to my section. I shouted at the top of my voice for them to come out. For a moment or two nothing happened. Then from the end of the buildings there appeared two of the oldest and scruffiest Germans I had ever seen, and although the section waited expectantly no more appeared. McVeigh's reaction was one of annoyance.

"'Ave I just gone through all I 'ave done for them ole goats?"

"We'd better look and see if there's any more," I said.

A search of the buildings produced a nil result, so the section took up a position beyond them and waited for the rest of the unit to arrive.

When they did, there was great excitement, for while we had been advancing on the huts, Guy Vourch with his French troop in the wood had taken a prisoner who had volunteered the information that the garrison of Vrouwenpolder was simply waiting to give itself up, and that if someone went forward, the place could be taken without any bloodshed on either side. After a certain amount of negotiation, Ken Wright, the Intelligence Officer had gone on in a jeep to the town to find out what the situation really was, and they were now awaiting his return, or some sort of message. Nor did we have long to wait. After about a quarter of an hour the jeep came back with a message to say we should make preparations to disarm and guard about a thousand or so prisoners, who would march in by companies complete with their arms and equipment. A few minutes later the first company arrived.

In all, there were fourteen hundred prisoners by the end of the afternoon. Vrouwenpolder was occupied by the Commando, and the battle of Walcheren was at an end.

CHAPTER VIII

Our deeds still travel with us from afar
And what we have been, makes us what we are.

GEORGE ELIOT

F OR No. 4, the operation on Walcheren was the last major
operation of the war. Not for us the Rhine crossing, nor
the final sweep into Germany; by that time the crest of the
wave had swept past us. It is true, during the remainder of
the winter of 1944-5 we carried out small-scale raids and
patrols amongst the islands of the Scheldt, our tactical role
being to prevent any German counter-thrust from the
north-west against Antwerp, but we were in a backwater of
the main stream of the war.

After the Flushing attack, Denny Rewcastle was recommended for the D.S.O. as he had been so largely instru-
mental in bringing about the success of the operation, but
after passing through the various stages on its journey to
Army H.Q., the award was reduced and further reduced,
until eventually Field-Marshal Montgomery was pleased to
award a Certificate of Merit for the services rendered. A
chap in the Army Postal Group in England got the same
award on the same day for sending out the mail.

Until March, 1945, we were stationed on North Beve-
land, patrolling on to the next island. Thence we moved to
the mainland and the end of hostilities found us near
Bergen op-Zoom.

In June, 1945, we were moved into Germany to
Recklinghausen in the Ruhr. There our duties were
guarding a prison camp, and there the unit began to split.

First of all, the French troops were sent back to France.
For most of them there followed a time of difficulty and dis-
satisfaction. They had been away from home so long that
they found themselves strangers, at least to the way of think-

ing which prevailed in their disrupted country. They found themselves working alongside and under Vichyites who lost no opportunity to have them shown up as hotheaded trouble-makers. It was a disappointing homecoming for many of them.

Guy Vourch began his studies again in Paris. He, too, was distressed by the attitude of his countrymen, but he reasoned that it was an aftermath of war and threw himself into his work so that he had the less time for worry. In Brigitte he found all the encouragement he required. I saw them both in Paris when part of the Commando was there at a celebration parade, and was delighted at the change in Guy. No longer was he an exile with worry on his mind and dark purpose in his eyes; quiet still, the intense look had left his face, his expression was that of a man who saw a future.

Phillippe Kieffer took the plunge into politics, where amidst the frustration and disunity he found at least something to aim at, some goal worth striving for.

Back in Germany, I was detached from the unit along with Ken Wright, the Intelligence Officer, to form an interrogation team with ten members of No. 10 Inter-allied Commando. These ten were all N.C.O.s or private soldiers, mostly from Germany themselves. They had been sent away by their parents before the war, when political pressure had made their homes unsafe. Then they had been boys. Now they had returned to the country of their birth, men, whose parents had disappeared into the limbo of the lost at Belsen, Buchenwald or any of the other hells constructed by Germany's Iron Men.

There were two P.O.W. camps containing in all some 250,000 prisoners of all ranks and categories. These we had first of all to sort out into groups—the sick, the S.S., the foreigners, the Germans—before we could start interrogation. The units guarding the camps spent days sifting groups from one compound to another to make easier the task of differentiation. Then we began the interrogation itself. It was a depressing business, for every normal healthy soldier

206

there seemed to be half a dozen warped or crippled in some way or other.

Many had T.B., the majority had dysentery, many had lost limbs, yet these ills were trivial compared with the disease of the mind, from which so many suffered. For many of them had been guards in one or other of the concentration camps, and these were scarcely men at all. Some had been doctors in these camps, carrying out experiments "in the cause of science." Many of the S.S. were still arrogant, contemptuous. Some were wanted men, to be held on charges of war crimes.

On the other hand were the broken bits of humanity whose lives had been wrecked by the war, men of mixed parentage, dragged into the German Army as "class 2" Germans, who had fought against relatives, friends, brothers, and who now had neither home, family nor nationality.

For two whole months we worked every day in this sickening mass of festering humanity. I was filled with admiration for the clear thinking and dispassionate judgment shown by Ken Wright in all the turmoil of our task. Small in stature, immense in his perspective, he organized the filing system, the reports, the removal and forwarding of wanted men to the appropriate headquarters, and was in charge of the actual interrogation at one camp, while I was at the other.

I was more than glad when we had finished the whole job though, and could return to the cleaner atmosphere of our own unit.

Soon, however, the early demob groups were called, and made their joyous re-entry into civvy street. With them went Len Coulson, who had been my best friend from the time I had joined the unit, a man whom I know better than any other man on earth; along with Peter Mercer-Wilson we had shared billets together, we had trained together, soldiered together. We had faced danger together, then when Peter had gone we still stuck together. It had been a long road.

Len went back to his native Northumberland to a job hardly commensurate with his stature and ability, there to wrest a living from an unsympathetic world.

One demob group went off after another, and the unit gradually disintegrated, until in March, 1946, we were officially disbanded, and those men that were left were sent back to their own units, frequently to the depots they had left years before, there to be given fatigue duties by the men who had never left the depot.

The war is over now, and we occasionally have reunions. We even returned as a unit to Flushing to unveil a memorial there, and every man took up just where he had left off, so that for a short time No. 4 Commando was re-born.

I like to think of the unit at a time when it was still a fighting force, when we stood with achievement behind us and looked with hope ahead, and there can be no better epitaph for any unit than the words used on a certain memorable occasion by Derek Mills-Roberts, who from a few days after D-day was Brigadier of the First Special Service Brigade:

"Men may forget, *you* may forget, but God will remember...."